# AT WAR WITHOUT WEAPONS

# AT WAR WITHOUT WEAPONS

## A PEACE-KEEPER IN THE BOSNIAN CONFLICT

## S.B. HUSUM

**Airlife**
England

The author would like to thank the Nykredits Fund and the Queen Margrethes and Prince Henriks Fund for financing the translation of this book.

Copyright © 1998 Søren Bo Husum

First published in the UK in 1998 by Airlife Publishing Ltd

Danish Edition first published in 1995 as 'I KRIG UDEN VÅBEN' by Bogan's Forlag, Lynge.

**British Library Cataloguing-in-Publication Data**
 A catalogue record for this book
 is available from the British Library

English translation by Tony Wedgwood.

ISBN 1 85310 998 3

Typeset by Phoenix Typesetting, Ilkley, West Yorkshire, England.
Printed in England by Biddles Ltd, Guildford and King's Lynn

**Airlife Publishing Ltd**
101 Longden Road, Shrewsbury, SY3 9EB, England

# *Foreword*

Foreword to the original Danish edition
by Denmark's Minister of Defence

The necessity of the UN's presence and work in former Yugoslavia is without question. The more than two million empty bellies that the UN helps fill is reason enough. But running refugee camps, keeping the conflicting parties apart and monitoring their actions is also an important part of it.

In Denmark, democracy and human rights are part and parcel of everyday life, so the decision to contribute towards the international effort in that country was not a difficult one. It was, quite simply, a moral obligation. But action must follow words and without the efforts of unselfish volunteers, such attempts would be doomed to failure.

For this reason, *At War Without Weapons* is an important book.

The synthesis of individual will and collective strength, the greatest single factor of being determined to make a difference, stands out from its pages. Without this attitude, how would the UN operate?

Any volunteer to former Yugoslavia is confronted with the peculiar, and for us frustrating, 'Balkan Logic' that abounds in the region. A form of twisted logic that has scarred the minds of all it has touched. A logic that makes friend fight friend, neighbour fight neighbour and father fight son. To western culture, such logic is almost incomprehensible but everyone serving in the UN in former Yugoslavia has had to absorb it and work according to it.

Søren Bo Husum does this with exemplary style.

He gives the reader a glimpse into the tribulations and hardship of a UN volunteer – from his anxious but excited farewells to his family to his mature and confident analysis of the situation after his homecoming, when the absurdities of what he went through assumed their proper perspective.

The book is an excellent introduction to everyday life as a UN volunteer. It provides invaluable background material for their families and friends, for those about to depart or for those curious to know what the tangible results of Denmark's UN policies may involve.

'When will it all end?' asks Rabia towards the end of the book, when her husband leaves for the front. When we know the answer to that question, we will know we have been of some use. Until then, we can read *At War Without Weapons* and be happy there are people who want to make a difference.

Hans Hækkerup
Minister of Defence

# *Contents*

Maps

# Introduction

In early August 1992, when the war in former Yugoslavia was still in its infancy, I was on a weekend's training with the Royal Hussar Regiment in which I was Captain in the Reserves. I got talking to a fellow officer who had just returned from six months' service as an EC monitor in that country. As he talked, it was as if the scales fell from my eyes – he was describing the challenge I had been searching for. From that instant in time, frozen in my memory for eternity, I knew I would never be at peace with myself until I, too, had made my contribution to that mission of which the UN was the spearhead. It was a calling that was not without problems. At 27, I was three years under the age limit for training as a UN observer. But I refused to give up, made incessant phone calls for months on end and pestered the authorities to make an exception. Meanwhile, events overtook me. The Ministry of Defence was finding it difficult to find (forgive the expression) older officers who were willing to volunteer. I was in – and after a three-week course in Finland, I was accepted as 'qualified for service' on 25 April 1993, my 28th birthday. My sister summed up the family's reaction with the laconic, though concerned, words 'Well, at least he made 28'.

This book is my personal account of the war which, when it started was on everybody's lips, but became more and more incomprehensible to more and more people. It is an account far removed from the seats of power in Geneva and other places where politicians have tried to produce an easily-digestible thumbnail sketch for consumption by the general public.

It is an account from the front line, where people fight and freeze, feel hungry and lonely, suffer and die. It is a kaleidoscopic documentary account of the war I was so close to for nine months as a United Nations Military Observer in former Yugoslavia.

It is also a small piece of military history that may help the reader piece together in his own mind what actually happened in a war where neighbours, friends and even brothers met in mortal combat with a ferocity few believed possible.

I had decided in advance that from the day of my arrival my observations would be recorded as material for this book. I meticulously kept a diary that ended up filling 750 pages and which was of enormous value in relating the moods and details that make the book such a personal recollection of historic events.

The book consists of a number of chapters in chronological order of what I experienced from my arrival on 25 April 1993 to my departure on 29 January 1994. In the first three months, I served in and around Mostar, the capital of Herzegovina, followed by three months on the coast of Croatia and spent the last three months in the Bihac Pocket. Little did I know at the time, but I was to find myself in the very worst hot-spots of the conflict and come eyeball to eyeball with the horror that is war. The book describes incidents of unfathomable destruction, human suffering, war crimes, personal danger and death. But it also tells of unbreakable friendships, warmth of spirit, undaunted courage, hope and happiness.

One of the abbreviations used often in the book is UNMO (United Nations Military Observer) a member of the military corps of observers belonging to the UN contingent called UNPROFOR (United Nations Protection Forces). It was to this corps I was attached. It consisted of 450 officers from 30 countries. The 'mission area', as former Yugoslavia was called, was divided into a number of sectors, manned by between 30 and 100 observers operating in teams of 5 to 15. We were unarmed, patrolled in unarmoured vehicles and, more often than not, quartered in private homes with the local population close to the front line. We received a lodgings allowance direct from the UN and therefore operated independently, logistically speaking, of the UN forces in the area. Our primary objective on paper was to monitor the observance of ceasefires. As there were no true ceasefires and those that were instituted were never respected, we were tasked to a variety of other duties that depended entirely on the conditions prevailing in the area in which we were at the time. But whatever we found ourselves doing, observing was central to our work. Because of our mobility, we were often dispatched as 'the first eyewitnesses' to events as they unfolded.

The book contains candid opinions of the incidents and atrocities I experienced. I owe as much to the people they touched. It is not, nor should it be interpreted as, a definitive accusation against any of the conflicting parties as being heroes or villains, murderers or victims. The situation in this war was far too complex to make such generalisations, even though I saw a great deal, though not everything, at first hand. It is first and foremost an account of what I saw, as a Danish officer in the service of the United Nations, with my own eyes.

It would be a major error to attribute the cause of this war entirely to the events surrounding the fragmentation of Yugoslavia in 1991. The country was a federation of population groups that go back more than a thousand years in history and the real cause of outbreak of war lies just as much with the tensions and contradictions that existed between them. It is a highly complex subject and beyond the scope of this book but where necessary I have given a basic explanation of the historical background to make the events I experienced understandable. But to set the scene, as it were, a summary of the major events that preceded this war would not be out of place in an introduction to the book.

The fragmentation of Yugoslavia gathered pace in 1991, when the parliaments in Slovenia and Croatia decided to break away from the federation and declare their former republics independent. The governments of western Europe were quick to recognise their autonomy but the large minority of Serbs in Croatia refused to accept that the ties to their Serbian brothers in Bosnia-Herzegovina and Serbia itself be broken. With the assistance of the Yugoslavian Federal Army, whose senior officers were predominantly Serbs, they spent the last six months of 1991 fighting for that third of Croatia which for generations had been inhabited by their forefathers and expelled all Croatians. These local Serbs wanted to create closer links with Serbia – to become part of a Serbian nation, a Greater Serbia. From the very beginnings of the conflict, international opinion was that existing borders should be maintained, and certainly not moved by armed force, and the action of the Serbs was universally condemned. Under international pressure, the conflicting parties entered a ceasefire, during which UN troops would be deployed in all the areas under Serb control. This deployment was to ensure three things: that the local Serbs laid down their arms and disbanded the military units in the territories under their control; that the Serbs should subsequently be able to live unmolested in Croatia, a condition the Zagreb government guaranteed in exchange for a certain degree of independence and which the UN would ensure happened by its presence for a limited period of time; that the expelled Croats could return to their homes and continue their lives as normal. For various reasons, the UN was unable to achieve any of these goals before the Croatian government ended the Serbian declaration of unilateral independence by force in August 1995 and put tens of thousands of Serbs to flight.

Meanwhile in Sarajevo, the parliament of Bosnia-Herzegovina followed Croatia and Slovenia in seceding from the federation and declared itself an independent nation.

In 1991, Bosnia-Herzegovina was 44% Muslim, 31% Serb, 17% Croat, 5.5% Yugoslav (people who regarded federal citizenship as the only citizenship that mattered) and 2.5% 'other'. The Serbs, primarily farmers, owned a disproportionate amount of the land. Quite how much is a good question – it depends on the sources of information and the statistical methods employed and varies from 40% to 64%.

The majority achieved in parliament came from the Muslim and Croat votes, with most of the Serbs voting against. At a referendum in the spring of 1993, the Muslim and Croat population affirmed parliament's decision whilst most of the Serbs refused to take part. They believed the parliamentary decision was in violation of the constitution, claiming such a momentous step as seceding from the federation, required the agreement of a majority of all three population groups. The Serbs simply refused to accept that they could be out-voted by a Muslim-Croat alliance. Their opponents, on the other hand, believed that the Serb interpretation of the constitution was incorrect and that secession could be achieved with a simple parliamentary majority confirmed by a referendum. Many countries hesitated to recognise the new nation, fearing that it would make the situation even more volatile. But with Germany and the USA at the forefront, Bosnia-Herzegovina quickly received international recognition as an independent state. The date of this recognition, 6 April, was a fateful day in the history of the failed federation. It also marked the liberation of Sarajevo in 1945 and the day of German invasion in 1941. The Serbs are a people very conscious of their past and perceived it as an insult that the international community made their recognition on that day of all days.

Shortly afterwards, the Bosnian Serbs took up arms they had acquired mainly from the Yugoslav army and in the space of just a few months took control of 65% of the country. The Muslims and Croats, united on Bosnia-Herzegovina's secession from the federation, were divided on its future. The Muslims wanted to preserve its status as a unified nation – the Croats wanted to form their own republic in the south, where they were in the majority, and then form a close alliance with Croatia. It was a serious conflict of interests that was ignored, temporarily at least, in favour of a marriage of convenience with military alliance as its dowry, allowing them to stand united against the Bosnian Serbs. Both the Muslims and the Croats were extremely poorly prepared for the bloody and merciless war that followed. The Muslims were in a particularly critical situation, with many of them trapped in defence pockets on both geographical sides of the country.

The UN mandate was now extended to include Bosnia-Herzegovina, where the primary objective was to ensure the safe passage of emergency supplies, most urgently to the enclaved Muslims. Its role was to be further expanded later but a final definition of how was never reached as events were constantly overtaken by local developments. A major military offensive intended to bring the war to an end was considered but quickly rejected. In the mountainous terrain, it would demand unlimited resources to bring such an operation to a successful conclusion, as the Germans discovered in World War II. Instead, the UN carried on with its balancing act, paying due respect to the historical and current interest of the major powers, as the war grew in ferocity and brutality.

There are undoubtedly many reasons, idealistic and pragmatic, for a number of countries electing to give active support to a peace-keeping mission, fully aware of the possible consequences for its own soldiers. The idealistic reasons may well be nothing more than a natural extension of the following declaration:

> No free man shall be taken or imprisoned or dispossessed,
> or outlawed or exiled, or in any way destroyed
> nor will we go upon him, nor will we send against him
> except by the lawful judgement of his peers
> or by the law of the land.
>
> Magna Carta, Clause 39.
> Signed by King John at Runnymede, 1215.

## Chapter 1

# Zagreb – A City Far From the War

I said goodbye to my family at Kastrup Airport in Copenhagen on 25 April 1993 – a beautiful spring day. The parting was not pleasant for any of us. My family was afraid it might be the last farewell and, for the very same reason, my conscience was tormenting me for putting my wishes above the needs of my loved ones. But my decision to go to the war zone was unshakeable and deep down I knew I did not really want it any other way. I felt a deep need to be a part of the history of the world that was being written in former Yugoslavia as I stood there. That I was doing so for an organisation that was working for a peaceful solution to the conflict made my need, in my eyes at least, legitimate. Even as I sat in the aircraft, I began to adjust my mind to the task ahead of me, a task which I imagined and, if I am honest with myself, hoped would be a tough and demanding challenge.

After landing at Zagreb airport, I was transported, together with six other Danish observers, to a former JNA[1] barracks near the centre of town, where UNPROFOR[2] had its headquarters. On the journey, we received countless fingers raised in derision and torrents of abuse from the people of the city, something which I learned was the daily greeting for UN personnel in the Croatian-controlled area. A large majority of the citizens of Croatia believed that UNPROFOR had not done enough to achieve that part of our mandate that, put simply, stated that Croatia should regain control of the geographical areas that had been in Serbian hands since the autumn of 1991.

The UNPROFOR headquarters was a veritable whirlwind of people – civilian and military, men and women, Africans, Arabs, South Americans, Asians and Europeans. The intensely international atmosphere that is part and parcel of a UN mission was immediately apparent. Tucked away in one corner of the barracks was the HQ for Military Observers. We were put through a four-day course before being sent out to our sectors, chosen to the basic tenet that there should be as few of the same nationality in the same sector as possible. The tests we had to take in that course included a language test and driving test, which presented few problems for the Scandinavian officers. For many of our future colleagues, however, especially those from Africa, they were not that easy. Most of them spoke good English, although with a very special form of pronunciation. When it came to driving, though, many of them took the instructor to the brink of a nervous breakdown because of their cavalier attitude to driving, which cost sundry dents and scratches on the cars he regarded as his own personal domain. The problem was, they were not used to sitting behind the wheel of their own private cars at home, where any officer with the least self-respect had his own chauffeur.

There was a large board hanging in the HQ, with passport-size photos of all the UNMOs, grouped by sector. My thoughts went to those colleagues I met on the course in Finland who were now serving in those areas where the action was still fiercest. I hoped soon to be following in their footsteps.

Placing the newly-arrived UNMOs in the various sectors was something of a jigsaw puzzle, with personal wishes varying greatly. The personnel officers were stormed by colleagues who wanted everything from a safe job in HQ to front-line action in Sarajevo. Enthusiasm ran highest among the young British officers who could not get into action fast enough. They verged on the hysterical if they were posted to a sector where their chances of close contact with the war they had come so far to be part of were poor. An English colleague from one of the cavalry regiments that recruited almost exclusively from the landed gentry later told me that it was simply socially unacceptable to return to his regiment without having experienced what it means to be at war. Preferably, you should go home having had a close shave somewhere and come through a dangerous situation by the skin of your teeth. So for him and many other British officers, the mission was just as much a question of gaining war experience as it was of performing humanitarian work. In my view, there is nothing odious in that as long as they did the job that was expected of them – which they did. But by traditional Danish standards, it would hardly be regarded as an acceptable motive for taking part in a UN mission.

16

Standing in the queue at the HQ cafeteria, I met a middle-aged Dutch major with a furrowed, rugged and suntanned face. On his chest he bore a 5×5 cm black metal shield, emblazoned with a lily and the inscription 'UNMO PAPA Sarajevo'. The undoubted intention was to signal to the world about him that he had served in one of the hot spots. PAPA was the code-name for the UNMOs who served in Sarajevo itself, an area under the control of the Bosnian Government Army. What he had to relate of events in that town were far from comforting trivialities and he pulled no punches in telling his tale. At first glance, he looked like the type who would enjoy giving a 'green' observer something to think about, so I remember taking his stories with a pinch of salt. Nonetheless, I wrote in my diary later the same day that if only half of what he said was true, this mission was going to be a lot different from what I had imagined in the comfort of my home. He told me that snipers from both sides regularly took pot-shots at UN observers, something which I found difficult to believe. I knew I had a chance of being in the wrong place at the wrong time and end up getting caught in shell-fire. But that we observers, for whose safety the warring partners had all given guarantees, should be walking about like so many moving targets just had to be an exaggeration of the truth. Nor had I ever heard anything about it in the Danish media and dismissed it out of hand. And swallowed hard.

That evening, the newly-arrived Danish contingent went into the centre of Zagreb. The town was humming with the hustle and bustle of any other large city in Europe in the summer. The innumerable pavement cafés buzzed with life and laughter, the shops bulged with goods and the inhabitants strolled around without a care in the world. The front line, which was static and had been for more than a year, was no more than 45 km from this scene of normality and Zagreb was easily within range of Serbian missiles. But so far, the realities of war had not forced themselves on the city and it had never been bombarded, which was obvious to even the casual observer. Nor was there even the slightest trace of precautionary protective modification to any of the buildings in the town. Zagreb was a city far from the war, both in distance and mentality, and had simply decided to ignore it. There were plenty of young men around, but you had to look hard to find one in uniform – and those that were struck me as being an undisciplined bunch. Many boasted designer stubble, scruffy uniforms and no headwear. Very different from the countless well-disciplined JNA conscripts I had seen in Belgrade in 1984, when I backpacked and Inter-Railed my way through Yugoslavia.

In the grandest square, right in the centre of town, a statue had been erected of Ban (Baron) Jelacic, an old Croatian folk hero, who had been banished during the Tito regime as an unacceptable symbol of nationalism. But with the death of socialism in Yugoslavia, the statue had been retrieved, cleaned up and erected once more for a new era of respect and glory. Every single trace of the political past had been erased with a thoroughness that sometimes verged on the comical. I bought a bar of chocolate produced for domestic consumption and the last word in the 'Made in Yugoslavia' message had been coyly covered with a small sticker saying, 'Croatia'.

This was the smallest example of a tidal wave of ethnic-nationalist awareness that swept through former Yugoslavia. Tito's communist brotherhood, that for almost half a century had screwed down the lid on the pressure cooker of historical tension, was now totally forgotten and replaced by the traditional virtues that had brought the peoples of the region in conflict so many times in the past. Through mass meetings and media campaigns, the individual population groups were reminded ceaselessly of the ethnic differences that were stifled in the Tito regime. The old national anthems were taken down from the shelves, dusted off and put to service once more in the name of the fatherland. New songs were written, and it was not uncommon for the messages of both new and old to be highly derogatory of the other ethnic groups. Children were taught to sing such songs. One was written during the most recent war and this, and others like it, laid down the firm foundation for the perpetuation of hatred among a new generation of children of war.

*The Ustasja[3] Lad*

From my mother, I learned to sing, 'Long Live Croatia'
From my aunt, I learned to chant, 'Fuck the Serbs'.

May a shell fall on every mother who does not give life to a son of Ante
May all of our mothers suffer death if in their life they do not cherish a
    son of Ante

May he die by his father's hand who refuses to acknowledge the return
    of the Blackshirts
Cry not, mother dear, nor besmirch my Ustasja blouse with your
    needless tears.

18

To the strains of the guitar, the kolo dancer whirls and
If you fool with the Croatians, you will pay dearly
Oh, Ustashe, when we turn against the Drina
To plant our feet on the soil of the fatherland!

The day after my arrival, I was informed by the Personnel Office that I was to serve in the southern sector in Bosnia-Herzegovina, a message which suited me fine. I had come here to do a job where it was most needed – and it looked like I was going to be doing just that. So it was with a heart full of noble expectation that I climbed aboard a Russian military transport aircraft on 29 April and set off for the Croatian coastal town of Split.

1. JNA *(Jugoslovenska Narodna Armija)*, the Yugoslav name for the Federal Yugoslav Army.
2. UNPROFOR (United Nations Protection Forces), the entire UN contingent in former Yugoslavia.
3. *Ustashe* was a Croatian fascist movement, active before and during World War II. The name, Ante, quoted in the song, refers to the leader of the *Ustashe*, Ante Pavelic, who, with the help of the Germans, governed a satellite puppet state consisting of today's Croatia and Bosnia-Herzegovina. The *Ustashe* were so ruthless in their crusade against the Serbian population that the German occupation troops had to intervene on many occasions and bring an end to the bloodbaths. The song is quoted from the Danish newspaper, *Politiken*, from 24 April 1993.

19

# Chapter 2

# Nevesinje – The Calm Before the Storm

O n the flight to Split, I met Roberto, an Argentinian Major serving in the Sector HQ. He was a big man, especially by South American standards, vaguely comical in his appearance, with a thick Hispanic accent, but there was a certain dignity about him. His stomach was impressive in its size and scope, as was his lovingly groomed moustache – both combined to make him a living caricature of a well-fed *patrone*, which was precisely what he was. He came from a wealthy family and owned a ranch and large areas of land in eastern Argentina. He had served in the Falklands War and gave a vivid and very entertaining account of how he was taken prisoner in the last few days of the conflict. It was done in the best British stiff-upper-lip manner by a young English soldier with the unforgettable words, 'Sir, I'm afraid I have to order you to lay down your pistol, sir!'

We were both picked up at the airport that evening and driven to Sector HQ in the Catholic stronghold of Medugorje, about 20 km south-west of the Herzegovinian capital, Mostar. Even though our journey was made in darkness, I got the impression that the destruction was far less extensive than I had expected. Ruined houses were few and far between and those I did see had obviously been demolished rather than bombarded. The explanation was simple – the war, raging 15 or 20 km away, had not yet arrived. Before the war, this area had been largely populated by Bosnian Croats who had quickly ensured effective control of this southerly corner of Bosnia-Herzegovina at its outbreak.

I did not get a chance to see much of the HQ. The very next morning, after a short briefing of the general situation by the Sector Commander, the SMO[1], I was instructed to get myself ready to be driven to the Bosnian Serbs' side of the front line. Here I was to join a team of observers called MX-1 in the town of Nevesinje, some 25 km east of Mostar. An agreement had been reached between the two parties of the conflict, the Bosnian Serbs on the one side and a coalition of Bosnian Croats and Muslims on the other, to keep a front-line corridor open for the UN to transport prisoners and casualties. The corridor ran through the town of Stolac, about 30 km south-east of Mostar, and as we got closer to the area, I saw the first tell-tale signs of battle. From 10 km away from the corridor, there was hardly a house left unscarred by explosions and the closer we got, the more extensive was the damage.

The road from Stolac to our lodgings in Nevesinje ran through a small town called Gacko where many of the residents shouted abuse and threw stones at our car. Before the war, there used to be a large Muslim minority that had been wiped out. The locals knew very well what the official views of the UN were of this incident and as a result we were regarded as unwelcome and nosy intruders. We were later to learn that this town was one of the very few where people were overtly hostile to UN representatives. The landscape in this south-easterly enclave of Bosnia-Herzegovina was beautiful, mountainous and fertile but lamentably backward in terms of development. Life in the small farming villages we passed through went on at its customary snail pace and little seemed to have changed for centuries.

Our new home town of Nevesinje had a population of about 11,000, one of the largest in the area. The houses were generally small and humble dwellings, the roads filthy and as full of holes as a Swiss cheese. The town was totally devoid of any charm or pulse, with nothing to offer any of the senses. The people bore the dull-ness of poverty and ignorance of the world beyond their mountains and yet deported themselves with pride and dignity. Surprisingly, they were friendly enough to us as individuals and to the UN as such, despite the stringent sanctions the Serbs were subject to. Superficially they seemed cold and aloof but if you made the effort to break the ice, their attitude changed magically and before you knew it your were being invited in for coffee or *slivovic*, the local plum brandy.

In the UNMO building I was quickly brought up to date on the situation in our area that covered 40 km of front line, which meant in this case that it was of Brigade status. When the other members of the team informed me we would not be taking part in anything that resembled front-line patrols, my disappointment was great, to put it mildly. This situation was relatively new – not so very long ago the cooperation between the UN and the Serbs had been excellent.

But since the Croatian attacks in 1993 on Serbs in various places in the areas under UN protection in Croatia (UNPAs[2]), the Bosnian Serbs had also acquired a deep mistrust of UNPROFOR and withheld their cooperation to the bare minimum. The fact that the attack need not have spoiled the relationship between the UN and the Bosnian Serbs, even in the slightest, was blithely ignored. To those people, a Serb was a Serb, even if he came from the dark side of the moon.

About all we were allowed to do was to make meaningless shopping trips in Montenegro's capital, Podgorica (formerly Titograd) and call on our colleagues in Ljubinje and Bileća, who were under the same tedious restrictions as us. So our physical presence was totally superfluous and was only maintained to prevent us losing all contact should the relationship improve in the future. For me, newly arrived, bursting with energy and keen to get to work, this situation was intolerable and I pulled every trick in the book in an attempt to come to an agreement with the local commandant on patrolling his section of the front. But it was to no avail. My efforts were fruitless and I soon abandoned my crusade.

One evening, we had the rare honour of a visit from the same commandant, a former JNA colonel who had been in action since the outbreak of the war and had led a brigade in the Battle of Vukovar. Colonel Gusic was a real tough guy, both in appearance and by nature. His ice-blue eyes had a magnetic attraction and when he spoke, slowly, firmly and with astonishing self-assurance, in a rich basso profundo, it was like listening to Moses after coming down the mountain. The man sitting opposite me was proud and decisive, but also stubborn and inflexible – the very archetype of the Bosnian Serb I was later to get to know. He did not give me the chance to say very much and steadfastly maintained that there could be no talk of re-introducing patrols until the UN was willing to extend some sign of goodwill to the Bosnian Serbs.

Confronted with such an uncompromising statement as that, my last, slim hope that we, as a team, might be able to make a breakthrough crumbled. What amazed me most of all was the fact that many of my colleagues seemed to enjoy the situation where there was nothing for them to do. They regarded it almost as a privilege that the UN was allowed to pay them for doing absolutely nothing. I could not begin to understand them and put their intransigence down to the fact that they had gone through some rough months in Sarajevo and regarded their time in Nevesinje as a period of rest and recreation.

We had a daily meeting with the brigade liaison officer to UNPROFOR, a likeable middle-aged man called Miroslav, who had been an officer in the reserve of the now disbanded JNA. These meetings were always very pleasant and equally unproductive. Neither of us had the power or authority necessary to grant permission for a new regime of patrols. As one day followed another in pointless succession, I became more and more desperate to do something worthwhile.

I almost pleaded with the SMO to be transferred to the other side of the front line, but my words fell on deaf ears and I had to reconcile myself to a prolonged period of mental torment. It was excruciatingly frustrating to be blocked at every turn in doing the job I had come to this troubled country to do. I was bored to distraction and had but one thought in my head – when would I be able to get out of this prison of thwarted expectations!

In May 1993, the Bosnian Serbs held a referendum on the Vance-Owen plan, which would create a united Bosnia-Herzegovina, divided into ten autonomous provinces by ethnic origin. The Muslims, Croats and Serbs would each govern three provinces, with Sarajevo coming under joint administration. There was a condition attached to the plan – that the Serbs were to withdraw from the extensive areas of territory they had occupied. The result of the referendum was a resounding NO, if my memory serves me correctly with an officially declared majority of 90%. For those of us living among the Serbs, this came as no surprise. It was blatantly and painfully obvious that only a pitifully small section of the population would accept the condition the plan demanded. Tired as they were of the war, if this was the alternative they would rather fight on. From our innumerable conversations with the local Bosnian Serbs, I had quickly come to realise that they lived in dread of losing their integrity, even their very existence as an ethnic group, if they became a minority in an autonomous country dominated by a Muslim/Croat coalition. This was a fear expressed by the housewife, the peasant, the private soldier and the brigade commander alike and was the prime reason given for the rejection of the Vance-Owen plan.

The foundation of this fear was a thousand years of political, cultural and religious contradiction which had been the source of regrettable and regular conflict in the Balkans. To the average Serb, this historical account had been a lengthy saga of recurring ordeals for the Serbian population. The German occupation in 1941, and even such distant events as the fateful battle against the Turks at Kosovo Polje in 1389, were rehashed with a vehemence that I found astonishing. To many, these ordeals were proof from God that the Serbs had a divine right to be where they were. By rational western European standards, there seems to be little logic attached to this belief, but this was the thinking of a majority of the Serbian population. Once the realisation of this driving force had sunk in, it became all too plain to me that the Serbian aggression which had led them to a provisional military victory was not just a question of creating Greater Serbia, the declared goal of the politicians. For the Serb on the street, it was merely a matter of successfully surviving yet another ordeal, a further trial by fire, that would ensure their continued viability. The political overlords in Belgrade exploited this historical bogeyman shamefully to further their own ambition.

Although this spectre of extinction was the prime reason for the rejection of the Vance-Owen plan, we heard other explanations that would make it far from simple to reach a peaceful solution. Our cleaning lady, who was otherwise completely uninterested in politics, voted against it because she could not accept that territory would have to be surrendered for which so many Serbian soldiers had died in order to secure. We asked her how she thought there could ever be an end to the war if all the partners counted their dead instead of their living. The only answer we received was a shrug of the shoulders.

At this time, there was also a lot of talk about NATO bombing Serbian artillery positions, including those ringing Sarajevo, if the Vance-Owen plan was not accepted. We spent some time discussing what would happen to us if this threat were put into action and were in no doubt that we would be in a very vulnerable position. We had learned enough of the Serbian mentality to know that as well-liked as we were as individuals, the locals would surely shoot us if their artillery positions were bombed. They might well do it with no feeling of hatred towards us and with tears in their eyes, but they would definitely do it. A Russian colleague told me that the 'it pains me to have to kill you' mentality was typical of the Slavs.

The brigade had a head of Military Police whose primary task seemed to be to ensure we respected the restrictions his chief had placed on our freedom of mobility. We had to have a pass even for the most trivial of errands. His zeal occasionally bordered on the paranoid, such as the time when he placed us under house arrest until he had investigated the suspicion he held that we were in radio contact with the fighters that regularly overflew the area as part of NATO's 'no flight zone'. Had he not had real power, and therefore an equally real capability of causing us harm, we would have laughed in his face instead of patiently trying to point out the absurdity of his accusations. News of our house arrest spread across our radio network and soon reached General Morillon[3] who demanded an explanation of General Mladic[4]. He passed the buck further until it ended up on the desk of the head of Military Police. The next day, it was a rather less confident man who informed us that 'despite first appearances, there were probably no real grounds for suspicion.'

One of my colleagues, Henry, was a very tall, very loquacious man of the Luo tribe of Kenya. His sense of humour was considerable and often employed, and divided his colleagues down the middle – you either found him hilariously funny or intensely irritating. He also achieved the impressive distinction of learning excellent Serbo-Croatian during the year he was a UNMO. When he walked the streets of town, the locals flocked round him as if he were a creature from outer space. Most of them had never seen a black man before and did not want to miss their chance. The children were even more curious, but even more wary of this man who was so conspicuous in the streets of their town. I look back on one incident with particular affection. One little chap overcame his fears enough to sidle up to Henry and reach out for his hand. When Henry took it in his, the little boy's face burst into a beaming smile, he snatched his hand away again and turned round with excitement to see whether the colour had rubbed off on him.

19 May turned out to be quite a special day. Henry and I were on our way home after a trip to Montenegro. Nothing much happened out of the ordinary until we reached the border of Bosnia-Herzegovina and were stopped by an officious Montenegran corporal who demanded, with a face like a thundercloud, to search our baggage. By UNPROFOR mandate, this was clearly unlawful, which we explained to him as we had to so many other guards. This man, though, was made of stronger stuff and his insistence became more and more aggressive, culminating in the drawing of his pistol. Looking down the barrel of a gun is always a convincing argument and this little corporal with a giant inferiority complex had his day of victory over the representatives of the gigantic organisation he so obviously disliked.

When we arrived in Nevesinje that afternoon, the local brigade asked us to visit two Bosnian-Croat soldiers who had been admitted to the town's hospital. They had recently been wounded in the serious fighting between Croats and Muslims that not long before had broken out all over Bosnia-Herzegovina. The hospital fell deplorably short of western standards, and was filthy and visibly unhygienic. People were smoking in the wards. The food was spartan and uninteresting – it looked like noodle soup, served with two chunks of white bread. But the hospital had one saving grace – it was far from the front line and was an enormous asset to the area. The meeting with the two wounded soldiers was an instructive, but far from pleasant, experience. We asked to be left alone with them, a request the Serbs granted.

One was a family man of 37 who had had a big toe and part of his foot amputated after being hit by shrapnel. He was enthusiastic about the treatment he had received and said that 'the Serbs were not nearly as bad as he had believed.' It all seemed a bit too rehearsed and unnatural to my ears. But on the other hand, he did not appear to be frightened or to have been abused.

The other man (24 years old) had been hit six days earlier by a 30-mm anti-aircraft shell that had shattered his left lower leg so badly it had to be amputated. He was timid, pale and thin, having lost a great deal of blood. His comments bore more the ring of truth and he claimed he had been fighting shoulder to shoulder with Serbian soldiers when he was wounded. We heard this piece of intelligence with a healthy share of scepticism though discovered later this was the norm in a war in which alliances were constantly changing and determined locally.

After talking with the two Croats for half an hour or so, three more male visitors arrived, all young and all in civilian clothes. I assumed they were friends from before the war but was told, to my amazement, that they did not know the two wounded at all, but had heard they were lying in hospital beds and had come to 'see if there was anything they needed'! To transform the scene into true theatre of the absurd, the young lads offered to return with cigarettes, apples and food the next day. My suspicions that we were being had were confirmed when Henry suddenly remembered where he had seen the three young men before. They were all policeman from the local nick, where our beloved head of Military Police was chief! His tasteless use of wounded soldiers for cheap propaganda was deplorable – and in true character. The incident, stupid and transparent as it was, reminded me of the bombing of the 'baby milk factory'[5] in the Gulf War.

The next day, 20 May during our meeting with the brigade liaison officer, we heard for the umpteenth time the saga of the righteous Serbs, fighting to hold off fundamentalist Muslims and fascist Croats. At that time, I had been in the area for only three weeks but had already grown tired of this daily dose of biased history. Little did I know that this was going to my daily bread for the entire nine months of my period of duty, whichever of the three sides I happened to be with.

The only difference in the stories was the reversal of roles of the heroes and villains. It was exceedingly tedious to listen to, but if we were to maintain constructive cooperation we had to put up with it. We had to appear interested in what was being said without paying it the slightest attention. We had to cultivate the art of listening without hearing.

On 22 May what I had been hoping against hope for actually happened. Because of the fighting then taking place in Mostar, the HQ in Medugorje needed immediate reinforcements. I volunteered on the spot, packed in five minutes, said goodbye to our liaison officer and interpreter and set out for the journey to Stolac and onwards to the HQ. Seldom have I breathed so sincere a sigh of relief as when I turned my back on the Bosnian Serb town where I had spent three wasted weeks. It was over and before me lay a real job, waiting to be done. Nevesinje was the calm before the storm.

---

1. SMO (Senior Military Observer), usually a major or lieutenant-colonel, the Commanding Officer of the UNMOs in a sector.
2. UNPAs (UN Protected Areas) were those areas of Croatia which local Serbs took by force in the autumn of 1991 and from which subsequently expelled all Croats. By mandate, and with UNPROFOR's help, the people were to receive assistance to return to their homeland. Up to the time of the Croatian major offensive in August 1995, this had still not happened.
3. General Morillon – Commander of the UN forces in Bosnia-Herzegovina in 1993.
4. General Ratko Mladic – Commander of the Bosnian-Serbian forces.
5. A blatant piece of Iraqi propaganda in which a sparkling new sign was planted in front of a bombed-out military factory in an effort to persuade the international press that the allies had bombed a baby milk factory.

## Chapter 3

# Mostar – Reality Far Beyond a Nightmare

No sooner had I arrived at HQ, not even yet billeted, before I was dispatched to patrol Mostar, together with Robert, a 24-year-old English major. An up-to-date situation report was needed of the fighting then taking place.

Mostar, the beautiful capital of the ancient principality of Herzegovina, is rather like a punch bowl ringed by mountains. The built-up area extends some $3 \times 4$ km, with a town centre of 2 km square tucked in the middle. The town is divided into two roughly equal parts by the Neretva river, running in a north-south direction, crossed by several bridges, most of which had been blown up. But the town's landmark, the 427-year-old Stari Most bridge still stood proudly in the very heart of the town. The houses near the old bridge were ancient and historic buildings, most of them between two and four storeys high. In the rest of town, the buildings were much newer and much taller. There was even the occasional steel and glass, American-inspired high-rise. Before the war, Mostar was a cosmopolitan town with a population of Serbs, Croats and Muslims in more or less equal numbers, and minority groups of Jews, gypsies and others. At the outbreak of the war, the Serbs had taken control of the eastern part of the town but were driven back in June 1992 by joint forces units of the HVO and Armija BiH[1]. Since then, the situation had been reasonably stable, with the exception of the regular Serbian bombardment of the town from the gun emplacements on the eastern mountain slopes. The alliance between the Croats and the Muslims that won the first battle of Mostar was beginning to creak under the strain, being held together more by necessity than inclination. Throughout April 1993, the relationship between the two partners deteriorated a little more with each passing day.

28

With the mutual blessings of Messrs Tudjman and Izetbegovic[2], the UN acted as intermediary in an attempt to cement the crumbling alliance – but the dice were cast. On 9 May 1993 Mostar exploded in a bloodbath, with Croats and Muslims at each others throats with unprecedented brutality, the two parties turning on each other as had happened in many places in Bosnia-Herzegovina. The second battle of Mostar was thus 14 days old when I headed for the town.

The journey was made at breakneck speed. Rob was a Royal Marine (a 'wet soldier' as I christened him) and drove like a madman, even when we reached the hairpin bends south-east of Mostar. My right foot had tried to push several holes through the bottom of the car on my side before I managed to beg him to slow down. Nevertheless, during this Hollywood car chase, I got enough glimpses of the area to realise that it was much more affluent than Nevesinje which was just 40 km away. Just before we reached the town, we stopped in a lay-by and donned flak jackets[3] and helmets and spent a few moments observing the town centre, shimmering in the baking sun. We could hear sporadic gunfire and saw a shell hit the roof of a house, causing a greyish white cloud of dust to plume upwards. We set off again, down the mountain road to the western part of the town. Halfway there, we were stopped at one of the countless HVO check-points and had to produce our ID cards before we were allowed to continue. They were not just picking on us, it was standard procedure for anyone wanting to enter or leave town. Mostar was a war zone and they were taking extra measures to ensure no undesirable individuals were allowed in and no men capable of fighting could escape.

As we drove along the main street of the western part of town, we could see few signs of the battle that was waging only 500 metres away. Because of the Muslim shortage of mortar ammunition, West Mostar was rarely subjected to the ordeal of high-trajectory fire[4], and it was not particularly dangerous to be in the main street and areas west of it. Amazing as it may sound, life in this part of town was fairly normal. It is true that many of the buildings were protected at street level against mortar shrapnel with buttresses of thick timber, and a good many windows were blown out. But the shops, restaurants and cafés, were open, and the people could move around pretty well unhindered by a war that was raging only half a kilometre from their doorsteps.

We stopped the car on one of the boulevardes leading to the heart of town and listened to the sounds of battle. The fighting did not sound too fierce and we continued on our way. A few minutes later, and I was at the front line, stunned by the enormous destruction that lay before my eyes. Everything, simply everything, was destroyed. Those houses that had not yet collapsed as a result of the murderous and incessant bombardment were gaping, empty shells, pitted with thousands and thousands of pockmarks from shrapnel and shells.

The streets were littered with bricks and masonry from the collapsed houses and in places were impassable. In whatever direction you looked, there were piles of broken belongings from what once were homes, tons of broken glass, fallen trees and telegraph poles, burned-out cars and, of course, countless shell cases, pieces of shrapnel and undetonated shells. The destruction was plainly recent and from repeated barrages, which magnified the feeling of shock. This scene from Armageddon in which I stood reminded me of pictures from Berlin and Dresden at the end of World War II. But the difference between a picture or a film and the reality of seeing such massive and extensive destruction with your own eyes, defies adequate description. Never in my life had I seen such horror.

There was an almost palpable tension and the butterflies in my stomach were fluttering wildly as we drove along the front line, which was relatively peaceful but almost audibly ticking the seconds away to the next wave of the inferno. Looking back on it, it was not the wisest thing to drive through the area in an unarmoured patrol car that was uncomfortably vulnerable to mortar fire and direct shooting. But at the time, we considered it a calculated risk, perhaps because nobody from our sector had yet been wounded, either by gunfire or shellfire. And anyway, I realised fairly quickly that dwelling too much on the thought of getting hit was a pointless exercise in an area like this and would be the inevitable precursor of a nervous breakdown. My way of coping with being on the front line was to believe we were invulnerable to shrapnel and invisible to snipers. Something of a fatalist attitude, I confess.

We continued towards the most forward of the Muslim positions, a few hundred metres from the west bank of the Neretva. The front line followed not the river but the streets and houses, which made the atmosphere tense enough to cut with a knife. In some places, the distance between the opposing front lines was terrifyingly small – sometimes the corner of a house. At one point, we rounded such a corner on Racina Street and stood suddenly face to face with a swarthy young Muslim soldier, barricaded behind a wall of sandbags. Whether he was an Arab or just looked like one, I do not know, but he could well have been a mujahedin, who both Serbs and Croats claimed were fighting in numbers on the side of the Muslims. Fear shone from his eyes, revealing a clear and understandable dread of what may be just around the corner in front of him. Nor were we that delighted to be suddenly looking down the barrel of a gun. After this incident, we always drove past that particular spot very slowly so as not to provoke a panic reaction that could prove fatal. A little further on I saw, for the very first time, the banner of the Armija BiH hanging over a street. It was a blue shield emblazoned with a white diagonal band with three lilies on each side. The lilies symbolised the three nationalities that make up Bosnia-Herzegovina – a noble gesture, using that traditional flag, especially with the Muslims now at war with the other two population groups.

Shortly afterwards, we crossed the Neretva river on the temporary Tito Bridge built by UNPROFOR at the end of the first Battle of Mostar. We now found ourselves in East Mostar, the Muslim strong-hold, and it was immediately apparent that reality here was very different from conditions in the main street of West Mostar, less than one kilometre away. Signs of the fighting were visible in all directions. Every house was peppered with shrapnel scars, there were shell holes in many of the roofs and there was not a single pane of glass in any of the windows. It was arrant nonsense to say we had left the front line. East Mostar received a daily battering by shells and heavy automatic weapons and of such ferocity that the rest of the area of this town was nothing less than an integral part of the front line. There was nowhere in town that could be regarded, even by the greatest optimist, as 'safe'. But the houses behind the central section of the front line were not in so sorry a state as those in the middle of no-man's-land, partly because the people had a will of iron, and the ability to match, and set to work repairing the damage immediately after a raid, fully aware that the next shell might fall in the space of a few minutes.

The Muslims were living in appalling conditions. Some 35,000 people were contained in an area no larger than $2 \times 3$ km. There was no electricity and no running water, which meant hygiene and sanitation were dreadful. There were two ways of obtaining water, both so fraught with danger for those brave (or desperate) enough to try, that water was a commodity worth its weight in gold. One potential source was the Neretva river in the middle of the front line, so those lion-hearts that did venture so far were a prime target for snipers. The other possibility was to fill tanks at one of the few public taps that were still operating. Those that tried their luck in this way also had to be wary of Croatian snipers, who had a clear line of fire to some of the taps and even if they did not, could always shoot people as they came running with their full tanks, scuttling across the streets facing west. Piles of refuse grew higher and higher and with temperatures of up to 35°C, the stench of decay and excrement lay across this part of town like a shroud. The first cases of typhus had already broken out. The military situation too appeared hopeless. The Muslims were fighting with their backs to the wall and whichever way they turned, they were surrounded. On the mountains to the east, there was the Serbian artillery, on the mountains to the west, north and south, the Croatian mortars. And to make matters worse, the mountains also bristled with anti-aircraft guns, with free line of fire over the entire eastern part of town, a fact the inhabitants were reminded of each and every day. In Mostar, all types of weapon were deployed against all types of target and the Geneva Convention was not worth the paper it was printed on.

The most grotesque sight of all was to see the people right up to 100 metres from the most forward Muslim positions walking, limping and running as they tried to make the most of their miserable existence, knowing they could fall victim at any time to a shell or one of the legion of snipers hiding in the high-rise buildings running from one end of the front line to the other – and on both sides. To see small children playing in the shelter of one side of the wall of a house whilst bullets and shrapnel thumped into the other side was something that was impossible to come to terms with, an absolute absurdity. My first dumbfounded reaction was to wonder how those children could even think of playing in a situation like this. But they really did seem to be enjoying themselves, all things considered, and even demonstrated their unconcern by waving at us cheerfully as we drove past. But the children were not alone in their astonishing demonstration of accepting their fate without losing their human spirit. Women, the elderly and even soldiers seemed to be coping with their tentative hold on life, a life that could be snuffed out like a candle at any moment by any of the innumerable shells that flew with unseen wings every day. The people of East Mostar simply refused to surrender.

We decided to take a drive round the neighbourhood, just to take the pulse of the situation. It did not take long – it did not take long to get anywhere in East Mostar. Off the Tito Bridge we took a right and drove along a narrow, cobble-stoned alley to the eastern quarter of the old town centre. Its ancient dignity and beauty had been despoiled and molested by the fighting that had destroyed many of the charming and historic buildings that had given it its character. The riverside houses facing the Neretva, in particular, were a sorry, tearful sight. The people here had lost the war of attrition – the snipers prevented them from repairing the damage of the bombardment. From here, we drove to the Ulica Marsala Tita, the Main Street of East Mostar, and passed a building that was an irresistible target for the Croatian mortars and cannons – the HQ of the Armija BiH in Herzegovina. The arterial street was jammed with people, passing the time in small, intimate groups on constant, but unapparent, watch against the shells that were uncaring for their targets in that quarter of town. Many of the children approached us to barter their way to cigarettes or sweets. They put us in something of a quandary. If we said no, we felt as if we were denying these poor people the most menial of luxuries in an otherwise comfortless existence. If we said yes, we were in danger of, in capitalist terminology, ruining the market, with every competitor starting a dumping campaign, and if you just gave it away, you ended up like the Pied Piper of Hamelin, with a train of 50 children tumbling in your wake.

Further up the street, there was a T-junction where a road led directly to the Tito Bridge. This crossroads was a Piccadilly Circus, encountered by many people on their way from north to south and south to north. Unfortunately for the Muslims, the Croatian snipers had a clear line of fire on this hustling and bustling thoroughfare from their Olympian lairs atop the bank on the west side. When a good and honest citizen was faced with the prospect of crossing this junction, he took a running start and sprinted, for all he was worth, the 30 metres before he was behind the shelter of the opposite corner of the street. But no matter how careful they were, no matter how closely they obeyed the 'game rules', this otherwise insignificant junction of two relatively minor roads was where most people met their death. One valiant soul with a well-developed social conscience had braved the statistically startling dangers and ventured out, presumably under the protective cover of darkness, to print a foreboding graffito on a wall in the snipers' line of fire. *'PAZI SNAJPER!'* (Beware Snipers!) – an eternal reminder that reality in East Mostar was, if you could ever doubt it, far beyond a nightmare. There were several other streets in this part of town that ran east-west which had to be negotiated in the same way if the people were not to be mown

33

down. The memory of running people, with their faces wide-eyed masks of fear, their lives dependent on their fleetness of foot, will remain with me forever.

On the other side of a T-junction a little further up the main street was East Mostar hospital, where all the wounded in this part of town were brought. A few hundred metres away and once more you were close to the front line, with the HVO-controlled 'Tihomer Mesic' barracks on the left and the completely demolished bus station on the right. If you were to continue 3 km north from here, you would arrive at the seriously damaged Mostar dam, also under HVO control. The road north was an alternative route into the town if the fighting around the Tito Bridge prevented its use. We did not take the dam road but turned right onto the mountain road that ran part way up the mountain-side. The houses here had suffered slightly less than those in the rest of town. As we drove south, we had a splendid panoramic view of the town centre to our right, with the distant mountain peaks forming a breathtaking backdrop. To our left, the houses continued up the mountain for a few hundred metres. From the last house, there was about 1 km to the top of the mountain, where the Serbs were polishing their guns and rubbing their hands in glee at the internal struggle that was weakening both their opponents to their own advantage. A couple of kilometres due south from here, there was another bridge over the Neretva, known to the UN as Pilot Bridge. This, the Mostar Dam and the Tito Bridge were the only possible ways for miles around to cross the river by car. We left the road before reaching the front line and followed a labyrinth of twisting and turning lanes and alleys, with the imposing bulk of Mount Hum always on our left, until we were back on Ulica Marsala Tita. The whole tour did not take long, and yet, in that short time, we had circumnavigated East Mostar, the Muslims' southern-most 'hedgehog nest' and one of the worst theatres of war in Bosnia-Herzegovina.

We now made for the Armija BiH HQ and walked into the Commandant's office with no difficulties, in fact without even having to produce our ID cards. The office was old, dirty and spartanly furnished with a desk, a small conference table and a few cupboards. Behind the desk on the wall, hung the flag of Bosnia-Herzegovina, next to a picture of General Sefer Halilovic, then supreme commander of Armija BiH. By no means a super-executive office but then elegance was an unaffordable luxury here in East Mostar. We were received by Esad Humo, second-in-command of 41

Brigade, known as the Mostar Brigade. This unit had the prime responsibility for the defence of East Mostar. Humo was an architect by profession and, apart from the usual national service, had no military education whatsoever. He made an immediate positive impression on me. He was a slender man in his early thirties, and his hazel eyes, slightly hooked nose and closely cropped black hair gave him the look of a Turk. He appeared intelligent and thoughtful and, unlike most, did not discuss in well-worn clichés but argued his point of view soundly and rationally. He put his case well but also expressed sympathy and understanding for some of the opinions of the two opposing parties, an extremely rare occurrence in this neck of the woods. Unlike most senior officers, he appreciated that our job consisted primarily of observation and arbitration. He had his doubts as to whether we would achieve anything but was prepared to give us the benefit of those doubts and promised his full cooperation if we reported our observations, and this was a true promise. It was no secret that the Armija BiH was hard pressed – they were so desperately short of weapons that they were handed over to the reliefs at the change of watch.

Our meeting was frequently interrupted by messengers arriving at the double. Humo would quickly evaluate the information, make a decision and send the messenger swiftly on his way back whence he came. What the contents of the messages were I have no way of knowing but unless they were all tedious trivia, he was unusually calm and collected in his decision-making. We were also rudely interrupted a couple of times by the Croatian bombardment of the HQ. Eyebrows rose to critical level when a mortar shell landed close enough to shake the walls and initiate an avalanche of plaster from the ceiling.

The meeting over, we gained a final impression of East Mostar before driving due north out of town through no-man's-land until we arrived at the HVO check-point, where the guards eyed us with obvious suspicion. They were amazed, to employ an understatement, that we patrolled the front line in an unarmoured vehicle. 'Don't you know there's a war on?' asked one of the guards rhetorically, to which we laconically replied that it had indeed not escaped our notice. The shaking of his head made me consider yet again whether our behaviour truly did border on insanity. And once more discard the notion on remembering the Croats really wanted us 'out of town before sun-up'. The guards now demanded to search our baggage to ensure we were not smuggling messages for the pinned-down and surrounded Muslim forces. Our first reaction was the same as that during the incident with the MP at Nevesinje – to burst out into hysterical laughter. But we bit our tongues again. Our authority was impressive, but remote – theirs was limited to automatic weapons but uncomfortably close to hand. Thankfully, we managed to convince them of our neutrality and we were sent on our way.

Back at our HQ we gave our sitrep (situation report), explaining that in the previous hours there had been small-arms fire that varied from the sporadic to the incessant and a certain amount of mortar fire. We could also report that there had been no movement of the front line in the previous 24 hours. As my head hit the pillow that night, bursting so much with the impressions received during the day that I had trouble falling asleep, I came to the conclusion that the task I had undertaken more than met my expectations for adventure and challenge.

The next two weeks saw us on daily patrols in Mostar, where the fighting and situation in the eastern sector of town deteriorated day by day.

Officially, a ceasefire agreed on 12 May 1993 was in force. Under its terms, the conflicting parties were to stop all hostilities, establish a de-militarised zone, permit a joint police force to patrol it and allow the two population groups free mobility between the two sides of town. This agreement was a UNPROFOR initiative and to ensure its implementation, a coordination committee had been formed, consisting of representatives of the two opposing parties and the UNPROFOR SMO, who acted as chairman. For almost three weeks, the SMO fought a brave fight at the daily meetings, acting as military midwife to the birth of the plan. But it was stillborn, doomed to failure from the outset. The Croats, who regarded Mostar as the capital of the future nation of the Bosnian Croats, *Herceg Bosna,* were not remotely interested in sharing their capital with Muslims, so they must take the lion's share of the blame for the failure of the plan. This was the first time, and unfortunately not the last, I went through a situation like this in former Yugoslavia, where despite the declaration of a ceasefire, fighting continued unabated.

Esad Humo once described the coordination committee as 'that three-ring circus where the Croats are trying to win time for their decisive attack on the eastern section of town'. As the words fell from his mouth, and as if by prior agreement, our meeting was interrupted by a highly excited man bursting into the office. He was one of the

Muslim delegates on the committee, which shortly before had been forcibly ejected both from the committee room and from West Mostar by the mayor. One of UNPROFOR's representatives had asked the mayor by what authority he had broken up the meeting. His reply was unanswerable, 'all the authority I need.' Until that meeting, this man had had nothing to do with the complex mechanisms underlying such a sensitive agreement and the fact the he was able to sabotage such a momentous meeting took my breath away. Anarchy ruled in Mostar!

The Muslims had felt threatened and in their haste to get out of West Mostar had forgotten a vehicle, one of East Mostar's few ambulances, which the Croats had given permission to transport civilians from west to east. The ambulance was still there, packed with women and children, deep in 'Indian territory'. We offered our assistance, arranged an escort consisting of ourselves and two APCs[5] from the Spanish UN battalion, who had a platoon permanently placed in East Mostar. As we reached the ambulance, we could see from some way off that it was peppered with bullet-holes and shrapnel, a collander on wheels, full of nervous and unhappy civilians who breathed an audible sigh of relief as we told them what was happening. We escorted them straight through the front line, across the Tito Bridge and into the eastern town, where we were greeted as heroes and guardian angels by the anxious waiting families, who, with tears coursing down their cheeks, blew us kisses and waved joyfully. This Red-Cross-type rescue mission was my first, but by no means the last. Because of the heavy fighting, UNPROFOR was the only one of the many international organisations in the area not to have scurried out of East Mostar. So apart from our real job of observing the military action, we also undertook missions that really lay in the aegis of the Red Cross and UNHCR (UN High Commission for Refugees). Over the next few weeks, we helped a great many civilians, both Muslims and Croats.

One such mission has printed itself indelibly in my memory. A young woman, four months pregnant, had to be rushed to hospital. Her baby had died and there was an acute need to remove it if infection and subsequent death were to be prevented. The hospital in East Mostar was not equipped to perform such an operation and the woman's only chance lay in being driven to the much better-equipped hospital in West Mostar. Together with an Argentinian colleague, I quickly arranged a meeting with the HVO, who allowed the woman to be transferred under the auspices of UNPROFOR.

With permission granted, we 'commandeered' the Spanish UN soldiers in East Mostar, who quickly had the patient admitted to hospital. These missions of mercy were really just a drop in the ocean, but they did allow us to make a humanitarian contribution and made us feel that our presence in the bedlam that was Mostar was visible and worthwhile. Our actions, which were often not without personal danger, also engendered a certain respect on both sides of the front line.

As easy as it was to build up a spirit of constructive cooperation with the Muslims, it was just as difficult to establish even the vestiges of a good relationship with the Croats. In East Mostar we could, at any time, even without prior arrangement, ask for a meeting with the brigade commander and, assuming he was available, have our request granted, but we never so much as exchanged a single word with Brigadier Lasic, commander of the HVO in Mostar. We saw him on numerous occasions, even sat in the same room, but he ignored us totally and utterly. To him, we were definitely *persona non grata*. Like the majority of his opponents in East Mostar, he was a 'hostilities only' officer, with no formal military education and, if the rumours were true, had been a waiter before the war.

As liaison officer, the HVO appointed a middle-aged, likeable and good-natured man who had been given no mandate for making decisions and reaching agreements on behalf of the HVO. Every time we presented him with a proposal or problem, he had to drop by a senior officer's office. That a man so junior in the HVO pecking order was appointed as our liaison officer was hardly a coincidence and reflected accurately how low a priority the Croats gave to contact with UNPROFOR. For them, we were little short of a bad conscience that heralded to the rest of the world what was really going on in Mostar. But despite the difficulties, we religiously maintained our daily contact with the HVO, not least to quell any unjustified accusations of being the 'Muslim observers'. Whether our welcome was warm or less than tepid, we bent over backwards to demonstrate our impartiality and share our time equally between the two parties.

On our way into West Mostar on the morning of 28 May we were stopped at an HVO check-point by a soldier bristling with weapons, who brusquely demanded to see our ID cards. With the sleeves and trouser legs of his uniform tightly rolled up, he looked like a military poseur, a Mostar Mardi Gras clown. With a subtle difference. Hanging off his body were not candy canes and toffee apples but grenades. After checking our identities, this little man received a nod of acceptance from another young soldier we assumed to be his elder brother, that was the open sesame allowing us to pass. We asked this young man's age but were sensible enough not to recommend another, more suitable playground, before we drove on to the middle of town. This valiant little warrior was all of eleven years old!

The war in Mostar appeared to have its own rhythm. We observed a daily pattern of the size and scope of the fighting. Until late morning, things were fairly quiet, with few mortar explosions and only sporadic firing along the front line. From then on, after lunch as it were, the fighting became more intensive hour by hour. It normally reached a peak in the late afternoon, when things really hotted up, with countless mortar shells every minute and continuous fire from small-arms and heavy machine-guns. Then there was a slow ebb until activity reached its nadir at about midnight.

This morning was no exception, with the town rather belatedly rubbing the sleep from its eyes. We crossed the front line, therefore, with no fears for our safety and drove over the Tito Bridge and into East Mostar. On the main street, near the T-junction immortalised by its *'PAZI SNAJPER!'* graffito, we ran into Humo, basking in the sunshine with a squad of soldiers from his brigade. We joined them and for a few blissful minutes forgot the war going on around us. But not for long. We heard the characteristic 'whoosh' followed by the roar of a mortar shell exploding two houses away – it brought us back to the harsh reality that we were on the front line of a war, not passing the time peacefully in a Parisian pavement café. We returned to the more sheltered surroundings of the Armija HQ. Here I met the brigade commander, a 40-year-old energetic fireball called Hujdur. He spoke no English and delegated primary contact with us to Humo. A little later, we met Arif Pasalic, then commander of the Armija BiH's 4th Corps[6], the massed Armija forces in the southerly part of Bosnia-Herzegovina. He was a tall, slim and distinguished middle-aged man who had been a colonel in the JNA. He struck me as being decisive but tired and weary of the great responsibility that had rested on his shoulders.

Just moving between the brigades of the Corps was a task confronted with enormous problems and required that he occasionally had to pass through HVO territory. As far as I could work out, he exercised his command throughout his dispersed units via coded radio messages. This can work for a short time but, in the long run, a military commander must have personal contact with his commanders in the field. In the second half of 1993, the chain of command in the Armija BiH HQ in Sarajevo was modified, so that units that were cut off and not in direct contact came under another army. Broken lines of communication were a not uncommon phenomenon for either HVO or Armija BiH, who had had countless small 'defence pockets' in enemy territory since the Croatians and Muslims had started fighting among themselves.

On the way out of the HQ, I heard a 'hello there' thrown in my direction, delivered with a decidedly native British accent. The man introduced himself as Norrie, a 58-year-old English volunteer/mercenary (which, depends on his motive for joining up) fighting on the side of the government. There were quite a few of these characters in former Yugoslavia. In the Armija BiH, they were mostly people from Muslim countries, but there was also a handful of Englishmen and Frenchmen. The HVO attracted mostly Germans, who were particularly popular with the Croats. The Bosnian Serbs' taste ran more to other Slavs, mostly Russians, and they recruited quite a number. The motivation of the various categories of volunteers to take part in another country's war varied from pure, unadulterated idealism to a simple quest for adventure. Norrie claimed he had come for the former reason because 'the people just deserve a better fate'. For the previous nine months, he had run a military training centre in Mostar for mixed Croat and Muslim units. Now he felt trapped by the fighting which he felt no desire to take part in.

I cannot be certain whether it was his fantasy or not, but he claimed to have a number of cloak-and-dagger missions under his belt. His mere presence in East Mostar would seem to indicate an element of truth but his stories were too fantastic to be believed. I think he was, in a nutshell, the last of the buccaneers, a man with an insatiable appetite for adventure, restless and without any perceptible roots. It was almost as if he had nothing to go home to, even though he had a daughter and a grandchild who doubtless mentioned him in their prayers. Two weeks later, he persuaded a group of journalists to smuggle him out in the boot of their car.

As the chimes of midnight tolled on 28 May the fighting, true to character, had intensified by the hour. The sound of automatic fire, from weapons of various calibres, echoed round the town. The mortars had now joined in the cacophony, claiming victims among the civilian population, especially among the Muslims. The mortar barrages were usually conducted as random fire, directed at no particular target and with a pattern that was both uncoordinated and unpredictable. Under heavy and continuous shelling, the people would normally seek shelter in their cellars, where they would be in relative safety. When shells fall out of the blue in a *blitz* attack, the fatalities can be high if there is a serious shortage of shelters. One tragic example of the havoc random fire can wreak was the single mortar shell that killed no less than 68 people in a Sarajevo market place on 5 February 1994.

We drove from the Armija BiH HQ to the suburb of Zalik in the north-easterly quarter of East Mostar, where the Croats asked us to investigate whether an elderly lady had been ill-treated by the Muslims. The road taking us there ran along the eastern slopes of the mountains, about 500 metres from the central section of the front line. To the anti-aircraft guns emplaced on the surrounding mountain tops, hitting a car in this stretch of road was like shooting ducks at a funfair. So despite all the guarantees for our safety issued from all sides, we took no chances and took this stretch flat out. Zalik, tucked into the steep slopes a kilometre from the Serbian positions, was as quiet as the grave. There was not a soul in sight and the only sign of life was the 'free-range' goats and chickens. After searching for some time, we unearthed a family, who, after a perfunctory introduction, cordially invited us in. The household consisted of a husband, wife, children and the husband's father, a mixed Muslim/Serb family, just one of thousands now in trouble because of the prevailing climate of ethnic division and animosity. The wife's entire family were Serbs and lived only a few kilometres away, though any form of contact was out of the question. They might as well have lived on Mars – not only because of the front line that ran between them but also because of the much more lethal minefield of their marriage, now an intolerable burden on the family ties.

Halil, the older man, cast his interested and inquisitive eyes over my uniform and remarked that it reminded him very much of one he had once worn. Then I knew what he had done in another life and it came as no surprise when he told me that, as a very young man, he had fought with the *Waffen-SS*. He had been through the hoop, from the major offensives on the Eastern Front to being captured by the British, thrown into a PoW camp and spending time in prison when he came home. As it turned out, a great many of the Muslim men I met in East Mostar had a past as German soldiers. When I asked them why they had joined up, most just shrugged their shoulders and flashed a crooked grin, as if to say it was something

41

they had not speculated too deeply about. When pressed, they admitted a variety of motivations, of which adventure and the fight against the *Cetniks*[7] were the most common. Halil knew the old Croatian lady we had come to visit quite well. He should – she was his neighbour. She was 85 years old and hard of hearing but we managed to ask her whether she wanted to be moved to the Croat quarter of town. She refused politely but firmly and shambled back to her little house. She seemed to have reached the stage in her life where what was going on in the world about her was a matter of complete indifference. We, however, had yet to be seduced into this state of utopia, so when we heard the smack of sniper bullets hitting the walls of a nearby house, we bade farewell to the family. They barricaded themselves behind their domestic walls, protected by the usual lengths of thick timber to catch the deadly hail of airborne projectiles. On our way down the mountain-side, the mortars opened up, exploding in our wake, soon followed by heavy showers of anti-aircraft shells. My guess was that the Croats were trying in a highly demonstrative way to rid themselves of one of the Muslim snipers that operated at various sites up the mountainside, including Zalik, from where they had a clear line of fire over all northern Mostar.

It was in this period, the last half of May 1993, that a series of strange occurrences between the two former allies took place. One of them was the Case of the Shuttle Buses. As already explained, the 12 May ceasefire brought agreement that the civilian population of Mostar could move unhindered between the two sides of town. For this purpose, a fleet of obsolete buses was made available to transport people across the front line. The Spanish UN battalion provided 2 APCs to escort them. The contrast between the merciless fighting being conducted by the opponents and the buses biding their time for a lull in the battle to transport people back and forth between friend and foe was bizarre, grotesque. Traffic came to a complete standstill after a bus filled with Muslims on the return journey to their homes in East Mostar was shot up by automatic weapons shortly before crossing the Neretva over the Tito Bridge. By a miracle, injury to those on board was purely superficial. This incident took place at much the same time as the final disintegration of the coordination committee. From the end of May, all dialogue between the Muslims and the Croats ceased to exist. From that moment, the war took a turn towards increased brutality, as impossible as it seemed at the time that it could be any cruder or more primitive than it already was.

Our day on 30 May started with a patrol of West Mostar, where a house on the main street had been razed to the ground during the night, with bricks, masonry and personal belongings scattered half across the road. As the house next door was still standing, only marred by old shrapnel damage, it was obvious this house had been blown up and not shelled, and in all probability belonged to a Serbian or Muslim family.

Ethnic 'cleansing' operations were carried out throughout former Yugoslavia and none of the three warring parties could deny having taken part to a greater or lesser extent. When a family had been scared out of their wits – and their homes – it was standard practice to demolish the house as a visible demonstration to the rest of the population that the eviction had been accomplished, a dotting of the i and a crossing of the t in that very word. The philosophy underlying this form of systematic destruction was that the family had lost a vital incentive to return to their old neighbourhood, as the last literally concrete link with it no longer existed. The logic in the thinking behind this Neanderthal behaviour evaporated with the inevitable realisation for all three opponents, but the Muslims and Croats in particular, that they were confronting insurmountable problems in re-housing their own people who had been evicted. The ensuing situation was over-filled houses where refugees were packed like battery hens into what houses remained, with piles of bricks and rubble as their silent and uncaring neighbours. It is beyond my imagination to believe that in these circumstances, such irrational actions were the responsibility of either civilian or military authorities. Demolition of houses in areas populated by their own refugees is much more likely to be the result of an organised campaign of pronounced civil disobedience.

To avoid unnecessary disturbance of the Brigade Commander's work, the Armija BiH appointed a liaison officer, just as the HVO had done. We had been warned this was to happen and as we could not always enjoy the services of one of the two interpreters in our HQ, we asked that, if it were at all possible, the officer concerned should be an English speaker. During a meeting with Esad Humo a few days later, we were introduced to a man who bore a looking-glass similarity to him and it came as little surprise to learn that it was, indeed, his younger brother. Seldom have I seen two brothers, even twins, look so much alike. His name was Mirza, but because of the Tweedledum-Tweedledee resemblance, we never called him

43

anything other than 'Young Humo'. He had been in action since the outbreak of war and it was with barely disguised pride that he told us of the June morning in 1992 when he and his compatriots had crossed the Neretva river in small boats and launched a surprise attack on the Serbs in East Mostar. He had been on the front line ever since, most recently in a special unit which he did not wish to describe in any more detail. During the day, he was at our disposal. But he could not do without the company of his former comrades in arms and at night returned to his unit.

The Humo brothers came from a very old and well-to-do family that had lived in Mostar for centuries and owned considerable property in the town and its suburbs. They made it quite plain that if they were to be forced from their ancestral home, it would be feet first. Surrender was unthinkable. They both held very strong beliefs in the Muslim right to live in Mostar, a belief that had little to do with religion as such. In fact, Young Humo once told me he was a devout atheist. They were shining examples of that section of the Muslim population who could see the reasonableness in some of the demands placed by the other two interested parties and who were therefore ready to negotiate. But if those negotiations should be conducted more in the spirit of dictatorial ultimatums, they were unconditionally prepared to die for their right to live where they wanted. Esad Humo put it succinctly, 'My family has lived in Mostar for 400 years. Should I really accept without resistance the Croats' demand to pack up and leave? Mostar is ours just as much as it is theirs and if they are not willing to share we are prepared to fight for our birthright. Make no mistake, we will fight to the very last man!' This resolve had roots that went deep into this mini-society and, outnumbered as they were, made this struggle a crusade against injustice. The word surrender was not in the vocabulary of the citizens of East Mostar.

The Muslims were literally fighting with their backs to the wall, a wall on which they had to keep a continually watchful eye, for in the mountains to the east the Serbs were waiting with bated breath to see what the outcome of this struggle would be. As the Serb Commander with responsibility for the Mostar theatre put it, 'what we are witnessing in Mostar right now is only the semi-final. We are still awaiting the winner.' That the Muslims were able to withstand such enormous pressure was a formidable performance which I respected greatly, without for a moment losing my essential impartiality. It was impossible not to admire the willpower, determination and acceptance of odds so heavily stacked against them that I observed amongst these proud people.

At the beginning of June, we reviewed our observations of the last couple of weeks, the evaluation of our daily patrols varying from two to six hours. We had to recognise that although we had a reasonably clear picture in parts, there were some pieces of the puzzle missing. We were, as the saying goes, looking through a glass, but darkly. It was quite apparent to us that the rest of the puzzle would fall into place if we could make our observations on a 24-hour basis. The SMO therefore asked the UN HQ in Kiseljak for their approval to set up a permanent observation team in Mostar. The first reaction was negative. HQ believed the UNMOs concerned would be too exposed by a permanent presence in the thick of the fighting. However, those of us in the sector HQ had a different opinion and after a lobbying tour to Kiseljak managed to convince our lords and masters of the sense and purpose of our plan. A week later approval was granted and we could start planning.

The first thing we had to decide was whether our future base should be in East or West Mostar. It did not take too much deliberation to select East Mostar, for two reasons: one, to ensure a permanent contact and fast response with the Armija BiH forces; two, an observation post on the mountain slopes of East Mostar would give us a grandstand view across almost the entire town and front line.

To amplify the first reason a little, if we were not physically in East Mostar any form of contact was impossible because of the broken lines of communication. But our HQ in Medugorje had telephone contact with the HVO around the clock.

We got in touch with Armija BiH to gain their official permission to establish a permanent observation team in that part of town and to seek their help in identifying a suitable building. With Esad Humo's assistance, we were offered the first floor of a house a little up the mountain-side which commanded a magnificent view and would make a splendid observation post. However, if our view of the fighting was good, then the view of our building from the cannon's mouth must inevitably be equally good. We would be sitting ducks. We were protected to some extent on each side by other buildings but the sloping terrain left us uncomfortably naked to any form of unpleasantness from the west, on all sides and from river level to mountain top.

The house was owned by the commanding officer of the Heavy

Mortars of the Armija BiH's 4th Corps[8] but occupied by his brother. Because of the acute shortage of suitable premises in East Mostar, we accepted the offer, despite our reservations arising from the matter of ownership, on the condition that we could have the entire first floor. We were very careful, from day one, to maintain a professional distance from the owner of the house, but our choice of a new observation post was later to put a strain on our relationship with the HVO.

Having found a home and office for the new observer team, we drove to the HVO HQ in West Mostar to bring them up to date. This time, however, we were met by an officer called Stanko Maric, who introduced himself as the third in the chain of command, without revealing what his area of responsibility, and therefore his role in the meeting, was. He was a large, heavily-built man, middle-aged with a provocative, joking air about him that made it difficult to know what he was really thinking.

I was to meet him several times later and gradually came to see that he acted as liaison officer with UNPROFOR in cases of principal importance. When we showed him the address of our new office, he gave a wry smile and said, 'Well, give Hasan my best regards'. As luck would have it, he and our future landlord were, at one and the same time, old friends and new enemies. Their friendship went back way before the war and was strengthened by the fact that they had both fought against the Serbs. I asked him how it was to be at war with a friend. After a short pause for thought and with a grin and a shrug of the shoulders, he answered, 'It's a bit like a boxer about to go into the ring. He can fight to win without feeling any malice towards his opponent and still be friends afterwards.' It struck me as being a bit medieval-romantic. The problem with this Sir Launcelot chivalry was that there might not be anybody left to be friends with. Every day proved to be the 'last round' for many soldiers on both sides. War is not for waging against friends. Friends are not for killing. On the other hand, I had to admit that the course of the war was not determined by men such as this HVO officer, who may only have been trying to make the best of a bad situation which he probably disliked intensely.

Back at Sector HQ, we put the finishing touches to our plans for the new team. The founding permanent members were only two in number – the New Zealander, Grant, inevitably known as Kiwi (after that country's national bird), who was team leader, and myself. We were to be supplemented by one or two officers from Medugorje

46

who would spend three or four days at a time in Mostar. The first of the augmentees was my Argentinian friend, Roberto. Until one was appointed at some unknown time in the future, we would have to make do without an interpreter. Such an appointment was a laborious and lengthy process in the hands of the civilian branch of the UN machine, which, at times, grinds exceeding slowly. As far as contact with the Muslims was concerned, this was no great problem as Young Humo, our new liaison officer, spoke excellent English. But with the Croats, we had to manage with German, sign language and the very basic interpreter capacity the HVO could muster.

By the evening of 5 June, our preparations were complete and we were ready the next morning to venture like pioneers into new and unknown territory. It took a long time to fall asleep that night. My brain was buzzing with a thousand thoughts. What will it be like to live there? What kind of reception would we be given? Would it have been better to have put me on the list of augmentee team members? The questions seemed countless and the answers few. I had made a decision whose consequences I was still not fully aware of, so perhaps the twinges of uncertainty I felt were only natural. But it was all very exciting and challenging and when I finally surrendered to sleep well after midnight, it was with a good conscience and relaxed feeling about the future. I was certain I had made the right decision.

---

1. HVO (*Hvratsko Vijece Obrane* – the Croatian Defence Council) – the army of the Bosnian Croats. Armija BiH (the army of Bosnia-Herzegovina) – the official army, that is, the army under the direct control of the government in Sarajevo. Manned almost entirely by Muslims.
2. Presidents of Croatia and Bosnia-Herzegovina respectively.
3. A flak jacket is made of kevlar and protects the upper part of the body against shrapnel and bullets up to a certain size. In the Danish model, there is a 30 × 30 cm ceramic plate to protect the chest against rounds from small-arms.
4. Fire from artillery and mortars.
5. APC (armoured personnel carrier) – with wheels or tracks to transport soldiers in safety in a combat area.
6. A Corps normally comprises a number of divisions formed from a number of brigades. In the 4th Corps, as in the other corps in Bosnia-Herzegovina, Muslim, Serbian and Croatian, the divisional link of the military hierarchy did not exist. Each brigade came directly under the Corps commanders.
7. *Cetnik* – (pronounced 'chetnik') – comes from the word *ceta*, meaning company. This was the name of the nationalist, royalist Serbs who, in World War II, organised themselves into 'companies' who fought against the occupying Germans for a Greater Serbia. Used in this war as a profanity for all Serbs.
8. The Heavy Mortars of the Armija BiH 4th Corps was apparently limited to a few mortars, with a serious shortage of ammunition at that.

# Chapter 4

# Mostar – 16 Days in Purgatory

After an uneventful journey, we arrived at the house in East Mostar on the morning of 6 June, with the car laden to the gunwales with food and equipment. We had barely managed to unload, before heavy fighting broke out in the centre of town. Before long, mortar shells were falling in other parts of town. Suddenly, three shells hit the unpaved road less than 50 metres from the house and shrapnel and stones were whistling past our ears. A moment later, the neighbour's house, 25 metres away, received a direct hit from a rocket-propelled grenade. At that time, the house had been our temporary quarters for less than an hour but it was already abundantly clear to us that we had not fully realised exactly what East Mostar had in store for us.

The shell that hit the neighbouring house killed a young woman, who was buried by her father the same afternoon in the back garden. The scene was set – and it did not change in all the time I lived in the town.

We were billeted on the first floor of the house, which looked much like all the others in the area: two-storeys, built of large, hollow red bricks, with a sloping roof. The house was about 600 metres from the central part of the front line and although it was scarred and all the windows were blown out, it bore no resemblance to the empty shells in the town centre. Propped against the empty windows on the ground floor facing west were massive beams, strategically placed to take most of the shrapnel that would otherwise have ricocheted around the downstairs rooms. The first floor, however, was completely unprotected. Shots could be fired directly into the house. Indeed, fire from heavy machine-guns could probably penetrate the walls. A mortar shell would undoubtedly cut through the roof like a knife through butter. The total lack of protection represented a deplorable and unacceptable increase in the risk to life and limb, which we immediately set to work to reduce to a minimum. The very same day, we requisitioned sandbags through the Spanish UN battalion. They were not working on the same time scale as us, however, and for the following week, we had to survive behind the thin, bare walls of the house. When the sandbags eventually arrived, we were faced with the Herculean task of filling them ourselves and putting them in place on the first floor. The work was done in baking heat and when we were finished, our hands were covered in blisters. Mostar was no place for the 'officer-and-gentleman' mentality and colonel had to sweat and toil as hard as corporal if he wanted to improve his chances of survival.

The first floor was barely suitable for habitation. There was a bathroom, though with no water, and no kitchen facilities. We had to carry water upstairs, a job which we accomplished at the rush as the staircase faced due west and was fully exposed to the snipers' bullets that were a daily threat to the civilian population. But having water at all was something of a luxury which we could enjoy simply because the house had its own well. We solved the cooking problem very neatly by taking our meals with the family downstairs. As payment, we provided them with all the food they needed, for them and us. My room was 3 × 3 metres, facing west, empty of furniture and devoid of any homely decoration on the walls. It was permanently gloomy because the shutters were closed to conceal our movement within the house. The only effects in the room were my camp bed and backpack, which was packed and ready to go in the event of an emergency evacuation. Although it does not sound particularly welcoming, I was very comfortable in our primitive and spartan home, where comradeship and fellowship more than made up for the lack of amenities.

The family downstairs welcomed us with overwhelming warmth and hospitality. In a place as raw and brutal as East Mostar, the need for human contact was paramount and the family provided that commodity to the full. Never in my life have I have been so spoiled. They were Muslims but with a very relaxed attitude towards their religion, a feeling I found to apply to most of the Muslims I met. The head of the household was Meho, the 40-year-old father, who was just as lean as his 35-year-old wife, Nedija, was plump. The pair of them were the epitome of kindness. They had two children, Aldin and Irma, aged ten and eight.

Also living on the ground floor were Meho's parents, who were refugees from a small village near Nevesinje. His father, Tehir, was a wonderful old man with a cunning smile. He, too, cast an eye over my uniform and nodded to himself in remembrance. As a very young man, he went to Spain and fought on the side of the government in the Spanish Civil War. When World War II reached the Balkans, he apparently had not had enough and he changed loyalties and reported to the *Waffen-SS 'Handzar'*[1] division and fought with them for three years with the rank of *Untersturmführer*, or lieutenant. He was decorated with the Iron Cross First Class and, unlike many veterans, managed to hang onto it, even during imprisonment and subsequent internment in his own country. But his prized medal, together with everything else he owned, was lost when he and his wife fled from Nevesinje. It was not difficult to see that his participation on the side of the Germans was more inspired by his insatiable spirit of adventure than political ideology.

The fighting on 6 June continued unabated throughout the day, with an intensity we had not seen before. From a west-facing window frame on the first floor of the house, we could observe the full extent of the action – fighting was in progress along virtually the entire front in the town centre. At that time, I had not yet learned to distinguish between the sounds of the various weapons and to me it was a deafening inferno of indefinable explosions and bursts of fire. My new-found Argentinian friend, Roberto, was invaluable – the Falklands War had taught him to recognise the sounds of all the weapons in the arsenal. This teddy bear of a man gave us a quick lecture, leaping about with wild gesticulations and giving a passable imitation of the sounds of the firing and detonation of all the weapons in use on the Mostar front line. It was a useful and hilarious lesson, made unforgettably vivid because of Roberto's effervescent personality. It came to an abrupt end, however, when he was upstaged by a 120-mm shell that landed so close to the house that the walls shook and we felt the shock wave in our stomachs.

That afternoon, I recorded an hour of the noise of battle on my Walkman as a reminder of the day when I experienced fighting at close-hand for the first time. When I replay that tape in the safety of my home and listen to the sounds of the continuous explosions, salvos of small-arms fire, countless shells and shrapnel hitting the house with a sickening crack or whistling past like an express train, I can hardly believe I experienced it at first-hand, let alone that I was relatively comfortable with it at the time. It is amazing what you can get used to when you have to.

With nightfall, there was, unusually, no sign that the fighting would abate, on the contrary. By nine o'clock, the action was so fierce it was impossible to make out single shots or even short bursts – it had developed into a deafening cacophony of automatic weapon fire. At times, mortar fire was so heavy that an explosion was heard every 15 seconds, mostly on the front line but also in the rest of town. At one point, we were contacted by Young Humo who believed that the intensity of the fighting could well be a precursor for a full-blown attack on the Muslim positions. It proved to be a false alarm.

The darkness transformed the battle being waged into a spectacular show. The night sky was laced with criss-crossing green arrows of tracer bullets. At the summit of Mount Hum to the south, there was a Croatian 40-mm Bofors anti-aircraft gun that sent an incessant shower of luminous green bursts of five shells towards the Muslim positions in the middle of town. This weapon, that was never silent, had a highly characteristic firing sequence – five dull thuds followed by five piercing explosions as the shells hit their target. And their target was the population, military as well as civilian, not exactly in accordance with the Geneva Convention but highly effective nonetheless. White flashes were seen all over town as the shells exploded. Close by the Tito Bridge, 200 metres of terraced houses were ablaze. Long yellowish red tongues of flame were racing out of the houses and up into the night sky, but quickly lost momentum and were swallowed up by the night. The darkness emphasised the impact of the fighting on both eyes and ears. As I sat there staring out into the night, I remembered for a moment how I had sat in my 2½ room flat in Copenhagen, gazing at the same night sky and collecting my thoughts as I put the final touches to my degree thesis. On that night in Mostar, it was impossibly difficult to imagine that that was only three months ago. The difference between the two worlds under the same sky was enormous. To sit in that dark room and observe the spectacular display of sound and light was exciting and magnificent. I was mesmerised by the sight that would not have been out of place in the finale of a Hollywood war epic.

A new day, 7 June, was but an hour old when we turned in for the night. For Grant and me, the experience was too vivid for us to be able to sleep. The situation was not helped any by the regular explosion of mortar shells. One direct hit on the roof and we were goners. If anyone had told me at the time that 16 days later, when I spent the night at the HQ, I would be unable to sleep because the mortars had stopped, I would have thought they were out of their minds. But that is precisely what happened. Difficult as Grant and I found it to drop off, Roberto had taken to his bunk and gone straight to sleep some hours ago and now lay dead to the world with his hands folded across his impressive stomach, sleeping like a big baby.

Gradually, tiredness overcame me but I was not to get a full night's sleep. At four in the morning, the artillery fire broke out once more in full voice. It gradually fell to a level that was merely loud by nine, when the day's fighting found its normal morning tempo. Roberto was irritatingly fresh and alert when he set out on the morning patrol with his two bleary-eyed colleagues.

The UN observers were not the only people working for humanitarian goals in Mostar. There were several other organisations, official and private, national and international, of varying sizes and professionalism. UNPROFOR, represented by the Spanish UN battalion and ourselves, was by far the largest and therefore the one regarded by the people as the primary assistance organisation. The Spanish battalion, for example, was responsible for escorting supply convoys to people in need in south and central Bosnia-Herzegovina. Among the other well-established organisations were UNHCR and the Red Cross. Apart from them, we often crossed paths with more or less privately financed organisations, some of whom, Doctors across Borders, for example, took their work very seriously. Others, however, were so amateur and ill-prepared that they were a liability to themselves and those about them. One classic example was a German who was so incensed by the pictures he saw on television that, out of his own pocket, he filled three trucks with food and blankets, drove them down to Bosnia and requested an UNPROFOR escort into the centre of the country, where he believed the need was greatest. He had no understanding of the complexities involved in food convoys, where the slightest mistake or inexactitude could hold up a convoy for days. Everybody would have been better served if he had donated the money to one of the recognised charity and aid organisations.

Getting emergency supplies to those people that really were in need was something of an art form and the convoy leaders had to be able to negotiate with both carrot and stick. It was not at all uncommon for a UN convoy to be faced with the demand that part of the load should be surrendered as payment for allowing it to pass and reach the most deprived areas. The UN was thus faced with the overriding decision as to whether to stop the convoys completely or accept this sordid trade in vital necessities. The option elected was the pragmatic one of leaving it to the convoy leaders to negotiate how large a portion of the load was to be delivered as ransom. The Red Cross, the other major organisation in the area, refused point blank to enter any such discussion and demanded that all loads arrived intact. The result was that their success was limited. They were geared to provide help in situations where war was waged in accordance with the accepted conventions. The trouble was that the only law that was respected in places like Mostar was the law of the jungle. From the wider point of view, including the ability to get supplies through in future conflicts, it is possible that the Red Cross, and not UNHCR, took the right stand. The UN runs the risk of opening a Pandora's Box if it even once condones the use of emergency supplies as barter. On the other hand, there was the consideration of hundreds of thousands of desperate people who would receive no help at all if cherished and honoured principles were rigidly maintained.

The problem of coordination was another obstacle we encountered in our work. Both the Spanish UN battalion and the white-liveried EC monitors[2] were trying to build up a picture of the military situation, as well as us. And when it came to humanitarian help, there were even more milling about. The parties waging war found it difficult to understand, not unreasonably, why we had made no coordination plans, removing the necessity for them to give the same information several times on the same day. As far as the Armijas were concerned, however, they would only be subjected to such dialogue twice a day, as we and the Spanish battalion were the only ones foolhardy enough to stay in East Mostar. We attempted to coordinate our activities with the Spanish on several occasions but constantly encountered problems that meant a certain amount of overlap was inevitable. In my opinion, these problems were symptomatic of the entire UN organisation. UNPROFOR sometimes seemed unmanageable, complicated and ineffective, which was highly irritating but hardly surprising, bearing in mind that it is a gigantic organisation comprised of people with widely differing ethnic, cultural and linguistic backgrounds, all trying to work together.

Our knowledge of the situation in Mostar improved day by day. Before long, we knew every nook and cranny of the town and of the front line in particular. We soon felt well qualified to arrive at an assessment of what was really happening. But Mostar was like a Russian doll and, almost daily, we were presented with a new element to understand in this complex war. One day, for example, we realised that the Serbs behind the mountains to the east were keeping Mostar on the boil by pumping mortar shells into East or West Mostar when the fighting died down. It was an effective tactic. The opponents played one off against the other and in no time the battle was raging at full strength again. Both the Croats and the Muslims knew what the Serbs were up to but could not afford to ignore it for the simple fact that it was not always them that initiated a flare-up during a lull in the fighting. At the level of the individual, too, I came across strange situations. Take Robert, for example. He was a Bosnian Croat and fighting for the Muslims. As a young national serviceman in the JNA, he saw action against his ethnic brothers in the battles of Osijek and Vukovar in the autumn of 1991.

When the war between the Croats and the Muslims broke out, he was put in another difficult situation, having to choose between his ethnic brothers and his best friend, a Muslim and, incidentally, son of Arif Pasalic. He chose his friend and, for the second time, found himself on the 'wrong' side of the front line. Robert, who was only twenty or so, already had a furrowed brow and tired, somewhat lifeless look in his eyes, for which he vehemently blamed the war. He was only one among many young men I met that had been prematurely aged by the ravages of war. I do not believe that taking part in a war is necessarily harmful to the psychological make-up of an otherwise well-balanced individual (as I said before, it is extraordinary what you can adapt to) but the physical price to be paid for being pushed to extremes (sleep deprivation, poor food, too many cigarettes and a great deal more) is high. The old adage about leaving home as a boy and returning as a man is very fitting to the youth who goes to war.

The children in particular had had their ability to grow and develop severely restricted with the outbreak of war. The very young probably did not really understand what was going on. Humo told me that his six-month-old son slept like a brick in their house just 150 metres from the front line. But the children old enough to want to play had very little opportunity. Not only did they stand the chance, like everyone else, of being hit by shrapnel, they had constantly to be aware of not presenting themselves to the snipers, who were seemingly not content with shooting enemy soldiers but anything else that moved or breathed. It was even claimed that children were a primary target as a hit attracted adults, the next target for the sniper's bullet. I never saw this loathsome tactic put into practice with my own eyes.

Just how dreadful the children's conditions for play were was brought home to me every day, just by watching Aldin and Irma from our house. From the front door, completely barricaded with massive beams, it was only about 15 metres to a brick garage that was the nearest place in the neighbourhood where children could play without being in the line of fire. When they wanted to play outdoors, they took a run-up and sprinted the 15 metres of the gravel path until they were safely in cover behind the garage. There they and the children next door played on their 15 square metres of waste ground until it was time to run the gauntlet in the flight across the street and home to safety. They could play there quite happily all day long, but when the fighting heated up and the shells began to get too close for comfort, their little playground was emptied as if by magic. For children, who really need to explore and discover, this situation must have been like a strait-jacket. Most of them were indeed affected by the situation and had, at a far too early age, learned what serious restriction of free mobility really means.

Apart from East Mostar the Muslims also controlled the village of Blagaj, 10 km to the south-east. Between the two, the Muslims controlled a narrow tongue of land with a paved road. In many places it was in direct line of sight of Croatian heavy machine-guns. The soldiers used Blagaj as a sort of area for rest and recreation. Not, by any means, because the village was spared the torment of war – people were killed every day – but for every twenty shells that fell on Mostar, only one fell on Blagaj. So, bearing in mind the fact that everything is relative, Blagaj could well be defined as a rest and recreation area. The journey between East Mostar and Blagaj was a dangerous one, especially in a car, where, on many stretches, you felt like the ducks at a funfair shooting gallery.

Hasan, who regularly inspected the positions in Blagaj, came perilously close on two occasions in as many weeks to becoming the ex-Commander of the Muslim mortars. On both occasions, his car was hit by a short burst from the Bofors on top of Mount Hum. What he was most upset about was the fact that his beloved and brand-new 4-wheel-drive vehicle was written off.

Grant and I once tried to drive to Blagaj to see for ourselves what the situation was. To avoid the funfair duck syndrome, we decided to take another and slightly longer route but had to give up when we were resolutely refused further passage at an HVO control post 2 km before the village.

On the way back to Mostar, we decided to drive to the HVO prisoner-of-war camp that had been established in a factory complex just south of the Hum mountain. It was not the first time we had tried to get inside that PoW camp, but at every attempt we had been refused admittance and without any powers of authority there was only one thing we could do – keep trying. As it turned out, this was to be our lucky day. The guards at the control post were conspicuous by their absence and we drove blithely past and into the camp. At first glance, it appeared abandoned, almost a ghost town. For ten minutes we drove between the rows of buildings without seeing sign of life. Then, suddenly, we were passing a long building in one corner of the camp with bars on the windows. Behind the bars were groups of men staring passively back at us as we drove past. Soon the windows were jammed with curious faces, though there was not a single attempt to make contact with us. From 30 metres away, they did not seem to have suffered any physical abuse or malnutrition. We considered talking to a couple prisoners ourselves but quickly dropped the idea as we knew full well that the HVO did not even want the Red Cross to visit the camp, though some weeks later the opportunity did present itself. Suddenly a guard doing his rounds spotted us. He was fighting a losing battle to conceal the astonishment that had frozen his face. How did we get in? Well, we took the road from the south. What were we doing here? We were doing our jobs, just as he was. A job, however, which came to an abrupt end as he hastily ordered us to be off the way we had come. When we came to the control post that had been empty on our arrival, the guards scowled at us as we passed. In the meantime, someone had apparently made them abundantly clear of the error of their ways, which may have been excused by the baking sun causing them to take shelter behind the guard post and lulling them to sleep in the absence of any stimulating activity. Despite frequent attempts thereafter, we never got inside that camp again.

9 June looked like being an unusually quiet day, with few mortar shells and only sporadic gunfire along the front line. Towards 3 o'clock, Grant and I were sitting in our room and observing from the window frame. The sun was shining and the birds were singing as they always did. Even when the fighting was at its heaviest, in the smallest of pauses in the symphony of war you could hear the cheerful twittering of little birds as they flitted from branch to branch, as a reminder to the warriors that the course of nature could not be disturbed by their brutal enterprise.

At 3 o'clock on the dot, the atmosphere changed abruptly. A six-storey block of flats some 800 metres from our house became the target for a heavy mortar attack. In the next four hours, more than 250 shells fell in an area no bigger than 400 × 800 metres. The Croatian anti-aircraft guns on the mountain-tops joined in and started the systematic shelling of Muslim strongholds in and around the houses along the front line. The Bofors on Mount Hum was particularly aggressive, sending salvo after salvo through the windows, destroying the interior of the houses and starting fires. After an hour of this blanket bombardment, three or four blocks of flats were in flames. Long, thick fingers of flame crawled up the walls, transforming the white houses into black, charred skeletons. Fire from small-arms was now so intense that there was hardly a break of more than five seconds. Not since our arrival on 6 June had we seen such fierce fighting. We were soon caught up, as we were three days ago, in the fighting but then if you stick your hand into a beehive, there is always a good chance you will be stung. As usual, the fighting soon spread to the whole town and throughout the afternoon, our house was repeatedly shaken by near misses, with stray shells and shrapnel whistling past our ears.

After many hours of this barrage, in which countless shells fell on the town, hostilities reached their usual 10 o'clock ebb. Once more we were free to move around the town, but by this time it was too late to get an impression of the seriousness of the damage. None of our neighbours had taken a direct hit but further down the mountain towards the centre of town a shell had fallen just outside a house and caused extensive damage. It was at times like this, I wondered why I had not been scared to death during the attack. We all knew what the outcome of a direct hit through the roof would be but I was truth-fully not afraid, strange as it may seem.

Like so many others in Mostar, I had got used to living with danger. It was probably around this time that I came to realise that man does not have a definitive and impassible psychological threshold. What we can cope with is simply a question of how successful we have been at mentally adjusting to a given situation. I am most certainly not the first to arrive at this conclusion but it was very rewarding to get there based on my own observations.

Not surprisingly, both the Armija BiH and HVO both had an explanation ready for the events of the previous night when we held our morning meetings at their respective HQs. Both blamed the other for starting the attack and claimed they had no alternative but to launch a counter-attack. This was a situation we faced every day as Military Observers, making our work a continual comparison of the claimed and the observed. We knew that one of the parties, perhaps even both, was being economical with the truth or even telling downright lies to put the other in a bad light. In normal circumstances, it might well be a source of irritation or discomfort to know bare-faced lies were being told to you. But it was simply part of the tactics employed by Croat, Muslim and Serb alike to gain the sympathy of the international community. We learned not to take it personally. But there was one thing the Croats and Muslims at least could reach agreement on – that despite the battle, the front line had not budged. Surprisingly enough, in more than six hours of fighting, there had been only two or three casualties in each side. In the light of the enormous consumption of ammunition, this was an amazingly low casualty rate, which led me to believe that they had just been trying to hold each other in check without any serious attempt to make a breakthrough. I once read that in Vietnam, 25,000 shots were fired for every soldier killed. This record was decidedly beaten in Mostar.

After the day's meeting, Grant and I decided to drive out to the area that had been the core of the battle to get a first-hand impression of the situation. It bore the unmistakable mark of death and destruction. We drove through the blackened piles of rubble without seeing a living soul. Suddenly a warning shot was fired at the car. This had happened before on our patrols. It was unpleasant but bearable, so long as they remained warning shots. We took the warning seriously and accelerated away from the emplacement that had shooed us off. As we drove off, we saw an unexploded hand grenade lying between lumps of fallen masonry but had no chance to take evasive action. Luckily for us, it did not go off. Unless you drove very slowly, which was hardly inviting in a place like this, such episodes were inevitable.

Despite its scarred brutality, the front line had a strong attraction. We looked upon it with a certain amount of awe as the place where you came face to face with the essential nature of war. Paradoxically, a patrol along the front line, with its display of death and destruction, was astonishingly refreshing and optimistic. It was certainly no pleasure tour through the area but the sheer, raw brutality of the place left you with an amazing sense of simply being alive. Emotions are known for blinding people to the obvious and we were well aware of the danger of letting our actions be dictated by our feelings. We made a pact that we would only patrol the front line when it was essential to our job.

On 11 June, something happened that was to make an irrevocable change to the way I looked upon our situation as UN troops.

Since the outbreak of hostilities the previous month, the humanitarian situation in East Mostar had deteriorated seriously. There was a shortage of just about everything but most importantly, water. The temporary hospital had reached its capacity in giving the wounded adequate treatment. Not only was it hopelessly under-equipped but supplies of medicine were running out and proper anaesthesia could no longer be given nor wounds treated effectively. The Armija BiH commanders therefore drew up a long list of essential requirements and appealed to the Red Cross, through UNPROFOR, for medical help. The Red Cross could not provide everything, far from it, but they could supply some essential drugs.

An application was made to HVO for permission to transfer the supplies. It was granted. We were not directly involved in this phase of the operation, so I cannot know whether the permission had the price tag of a return favour, in much the same way as the food convoys. Operational command was later given to the Spanish battalion and the date set for 11 June.

By 1800, we had completed the day's patrols and informed HQ in our daily sitrep that the day had been like most days in Mostar – regular bouts of small-arms and machine-gun fire interspersed with irregular waves of shells, both at the front line and in other areas of town. I was sitting in our room with Louis, the Venezuelan from the pool of rotating observers, observing the town centre, beautifully illuminated by the scorching afternoon sun. Louis was a helicopter pilot in the army and entertained me with blood-curdling stories of his countless sorties against Colombian drug bands that operated in the mountainous jungle regions between Colombia and Venezuela. At 1845, I saw a column of Spanish APCs crossing the Tito Bridge. One of the vehicles bore the mark of the Red Cross and no sooner had the thought crossed my mind that this was the day of the medicine convoy than heavy gunfire broke out among the APCs. The shooting was still continuing unabated when one of our field telephones suddenly burst into life. It was the Armija BiH HQ and at the other end of the line Young Humo told us that the Spanish platoon commander in charge of the escort had just been shot and was in hospital in East Mostar.

My first thought was, 'He can't be! This can't be happening!' I could not imagine in my wildest dreams that anyone could stoop so low as to open fire on the Spanish, particularly on an occasion such as this. We had to verify the information immediately, so a few minutes later Grant and Louis, dressed in battle helmets and flak jackets, were on the way to the hospital. Shortly afterwards, Grant called me on the radio and I could hear from the tone of his voice that he had bad news. I passed the sad message on to sector HQ in Medugorje, from where Roberto drove to the Spanish UN battalion and informed the commander personally. At that time, some thirty minutes had elapsed since the platoon commander had been shot and the battalion commander was blissfully ignorant of the whole situation when he greeted the big Argentinan. Roberto told me later that the man's face, sporting enormous bushy salt and pepper eyebrows, became as black as thunder and he thumped the table with his bare fist and, trembling with rage, roared, *'Putos!'* (sons of whores).

Back in Mostar, Grant and Louis were still upset by the episode when they got back to the house. They told me that the platoon commander, a young lieutenant of 26, had been shot through the open roof hatch of his APC. The bullet had hit him in the neck and continued through his entire torso. He was still alive when he reached hospital but died shortly afterwards. The Spanish soldiers at and near the hospital were, naturally enough, very agitated. A few weeks previously, another lieutenant had been killed by a piece of shrapnel in the neck when the hospital came under mortar fire. But the death of the latest victim was far worse as it was an act of premeditated murder, something which had not been seen before among the UN forces in Mostar. Shortly after the shooting, the Spanish responded with virtually every weapon they could muster. But they were shooting at thin air, as the killer, almost certainly a sniper, was not located. They considered instigating an immediate search of the area to find the culprit but wisely abandoned this hopeless task. Instead, they changed the wheel on one of the vehicles that had received numerous direct hits and returned the dead platoon commander to HQ in Medugorje for post mortem.

The killing had generated a feeling of listlessness among the UN observers. None of us had believed that we, as UN soldiers, should ever be the target for snipers. The fact that it had actually happened, sparked off an endless stream of unanswered questions. Could we believe that this was merely the independent deed of a single psychopath or was it but the first act of an organised campaign against UN soldiers? If it were, we observers in our unarmoured cars were inadequately equipped to patrol the town, to put it mildly. A discussion grew as to how we could clarify the situation and we arrived at the unhappy conclusion that the only way to find out was to get out onto the streets and see what happened. It left us all with an uncomfortable feeling that something was terribly wrong somewhere.

An investigation team from the Spanish battalion came to Mostar some time later to determine the circumstances surrounding the killing. To nobody's surprise, the Commanders of both Armija BiH and HVO denied any responsibility for the episode. The Spanish investigation pointed clearly to the fact that the lethal shot had been fired from the top of a tall bank building, from where the sniper had a clear line of fire to the place where the lieutenant was killed. The bank lay in HVO controlled territory.

At 2200 on that sad day of 11 June, we received another call from the Armija BiH HQ. It was a very out of breath and agitated Young Humo who reported, 'Many military cars and tanks coming from the HVO side, 150 metres on both sides of the river. Coming from the heliport[3]. Direction the city.' We barely had time to acknowledge before he hung up. It was unlike Young Humo to get excited without very good reason, so we grabbed the other field telephone to hear what HVO HQ had to say about the situation. The duty officer was unable to confirm our information.

The only area we were unable to see from the house was the southernmost tip of the town between the two mountains on each side of the Neretva, the precise location of the alleged attack that was about to happen. So we decided to find a suitable observation post elsewhere on the slope of the mountain. Grant and I tried to move downhill towards the south-west but were forced to turn back by shelling that had intensified in the last hour. East Mostar was also as black as pitch which made it difficult even to find our way. And using a torch was unthinkable because of the snipers. Back in the house once more, Meho said he knew of a good place further up the mountain. Grant, Louis, Meho and I set out once more, this time equipped with Nightvision[4] and portable radio, allowing us to stay in touch with HQ in Medugorje. Meho led us up the steep, pot-holed gravel trail, past one blackened and battered house after another, until we arrived at a white, two-storey concrete building 400 metres further up that was still under construction. The roof of the building served as an observation platform and we were apparently not the first to use it as such. An ingenious but rickety system of planks led to the top of the building. The view from the roof was stupendous, even better than from our house, but we were still unable to see the

whole area of interest. But having got thus far, we could just as well take a good look around. It was like sitting on the top row in the middle of a large football stadium.

The Bofors gun on Mount Hum was spewing its usual shower of green tracer on the town centre. There was a steady exchange of small-arms fire and occasional mortar fire, so everything was as normal. As we approached within a kilometre of the front line, the chatter was lively but it quickly became apparent, even when we took our first break, that this was hardly the place to enjoy a nice cosy evening together. We were surrounded by the short, high-pitched screams of ricocheting bullets and shrapnel at varying ranges. Quite why we did it I cannot remember but we responded by lying on our backs and gazing up at the crystal clear night sky studded with bright stars. It was beautiful and insane at the same time. We stayed like this for some time, saying not a word and just listening to the constant concerto of sounds of varying pitch and intensity, depending on the calibre of the weapon being fired. As we lay there, Medugorje called us on the radio.

The duty officer informed us that General Pellnäs, from the HQ in Zagreb, had given a personal order that we were only to leave our house if it were absolutely essential.

Pellnäs, the supreme commander of all Military Observers in former Yugoslavia, was clearly worried about the tragic events of the day. He was trying to make sure we did not suffer the same fate. We found his concern touching, even though we could barely keep the smiles from our faces at the situation we were in. I am sure that we all had the same thought – 'Little does he know'. After a while, it all became too much for Grant and in his New Zealand drawl he said, 'All right, mate, I've had it. Let's go'. The walk down the swaying planks did not have the same spirit of adventure as the climb up, probably because we were aware of the demons of the night that surrounded us on all sides.

On arrival back at the house, Nedija made a grab for the coffee grinder and swung the handle with such enthusiasm the sparks almost flew. We spent the rest of the evening together with the family, to whom we had grown very attached. That evening, Nedija tried to arouse my interest in one of the girls from the neighbourhood called Ramina, a tall well-developed 18-year-old, whom she thought would make a good match. She did it in an amusing way but I sensed nonetheless that she was serious behind the façade of fun. I told her that I had a girlfriend at home in Denmark, at which she looked at my ring finger and asked, 'Are you married?' 'No, I'm not but . . .' I was interrupted by a beaming smile and the exclamation, *'Nema problema!'* (No problem). Only a wedding ring would prevent her from playing Cupid and I could not fail to notice over the next few days that Ramina always seemed to be busily occupied with some domestic chore in the house whenever I happened to be around. 'She will make a good wife,' said Nedija, with a challenging glint in her eye.

We stayed up late that night so as not to be caught napping in the event of the HVO attack which Young Humo predicted but never actually came to anything. The next morning, we realised it was just another of the unfounded rumours that abounded in Mostar.

Two days later, on 13 June, I was witness to a trivial episode that illustrated all too clearly how little respect the partners in conflict had for each other. During the morning meeting with our kind but ineffectual Croatian liaison officer, he delivered a note addressed to 'The Muslim forces in Mostar', proposing a meeting between the two warring parties in the town. We were asked to deliver the note and I handed it to General Pasalic in person. His only reaction was a slight shaking of his head at the contents of the letter in general and the addressee in particular. At the bottom of the same piece of paper, Pasalic dictated a four-line answer that began with 'Addressee unknown' and continued, 'If you want to meet us, you will have to learn to call us by our correct names'. We were then asked to return the note to the HVO. Behind this apparently childish behaviour, there was a deep contempt and total lack of respect and flexibility. HVO claimed that after the break between them and Armija BiH, the soldiers of the Armija BiH were no longer Croats or Serbs, hence the term 'The Muslim forces'. Despite the fact that after the break the majority of the Armija BiH troops were indeed Muslims, the commanding officers refused point blank to allow their forces to be addressed in a manner they regarded as derogatory.

At first, we tried to persuade the HVO to call Armija BiH by its proper name – unsuccessfully. We then tried to persuade the Armija general staff, who had the official backing of Bosnia-Herzegovina and thereby the international community, to accept the letter, despite the unofficial title. All in an attempt at least to bring the parties to the table. But it was in vain. Neither of the parties had the will and we had to drop our plans and accept the fact that we were unlikely to change the course of the war. At the end of the day, I sat back with an unpleasant feeling that for all our good intentions we had been manipulated in a masquerade that was beneath the dignity of our mission. I promised myself that never again would I offer my services for such a farce.

On 14 June, Oleg, a Russian and a new member of the team, and I met Young Humo, who started off our meeting by announcing that that particular day was rather special. It marked the first anniversary of the all-out offensive on the Neretva, that ended with the Serbs being driven from the eastern sectors of the town. According to Humo, the shock troops in the force consisted mainly of units from the Armija BiH, with HVO troops primarily manning the support weapons and crossing the Neretva only after the Serbs were sent packing. He referred to the Croatian soldiers contemptuously as 'checkpoint soldiers', by which he meant that they were not 'real' soldiers but more like border guards. Not surprisingly, our Croatian liaison officer had a different story to tell about the attack when we met him later in the day. His version was that the attack had been led by HVO battalions, with the Muslims playing only a small part. Quite who was right I have no idea and it is of little interest. One thing, however, was plain to me – it was hardly surprising they could not agree to share the future when they could not even agree on the past.

The meeting with Young Humo changed to a more serious mood when he once again complained that Croatian snipers had shot and killed a civilian, this time a 7-year-old girl. Oleg and I decided that this time we would confirm the information and asked for permission to see the body. There was no real reason why we should not, provided that the funeral had not already taken place, which happened almost immediately because of the high temperatures. Before long, we were given the green light. The dead child was in the hospital's mortuary, set up in a squalid wooden shed just opposite the hospital. We were first taken to the hospital itself, as neither Oleg nor I had been inside it before.

The hospital was an old two-storey house in the patrician style, barricaded with timber and sandbags at every window. Though it lay a good 200 metres from the centre of the front line, it was a popular target for Croatian shells and badly damaged. In fact, it was barely possible to see the original red façade because of the white of the bricks and mortar revealed by countless shell holes. It was obvious at first glance that the building had not been a hospital before the war, a school perhaps or some other institution.

For the safety of the staff and patients, the actual hospital was set up in the cellars of the building, under extremely cramped conditions. The close encounter with the tragedies that had unfolded in this crowded crypt came as something of a shock for me. Never had the human costs of war been brought home to me with such stark reality as the sight that greeted me here. There were wounded everywhere, standing, sitting, lying down, in every room and in the passages between them. Some were screaming, some moaning, whilst others sat resignedly with a far-away look in their eyes and waited patiently to receive what emergency treatment they could be given. The characteristic smell of coagulated blood was unmistakable. There were pools of blood, fresh and clotted, on the floor, walls, doors and furniture. When there was time, it was wiped up with cloths already saturated in more blood. There was no water. Against the walls, were propped bloody stretchers which had transported the wounded down to the cellar and which might, at any moment, be used to take them up again – to the mortuary. The handful of doctors, who were inhumanly overworked, were constantly on the move, despite the fact that many of them appeared to be close to exhaustion. With their darkened and sunken blood-shot eyes, they looked more like patients than physicians. The hospital was hopelessly under-equipped with medicine and surgical instruments.

Shortly after we arrived, a 60-year-old woman was rushed in and put straight onto the operating table. An oxygen mask was put on her and the doctors began their examination. Others were called in to give assistance but they took one look and wrinkled their brows in doubt. From a distance there was not a drop of blood or a mark to be seen on her naked body. But when I went closer I could see a 2-cm bullet-hole in the left side of her forehead, with the surrounding flesh peeled back. It was a repellent sight that made me feel sick. To my amazement, she was still alive but the doctors apparently did not rate her chances very highly.

On the way out of the cellar, I saw the hospital's dentist. He appeared to be the least overworked member of the medical staff, which came as no surprise bearing in mind the fact that most people here do not have a tooth left in their head after the age of 30.

One of the doctors now took us over to the wooden shed opposite the hospital, where the dead of the previous day were kept. In the course of the day, they were all to be buried in the already crowded graveyards of East Mostar, established in one of the town's small parks. The only dead person I had seen in my life up to that point was my grandfather, who died of natural causes at a ripe old age. However, like everybody else, I had seen dead bodies on television, without it affecting me terribly. As I saw the wound in that woman's head, I realised that coming face to face with the dead and dying was a much grimmer experience than seeing it on a screen. Actually to stand in the middle of a tragedy, to listen to the terrified voices, to hear all the sounds and breathe in all the smells just cannot be compared to the impression left by a TV report.

It was not with the greatest will that I walked into the gloomy shed, still with a faint sensation of nausea. On the rough and filthy concrete floor there were four stretchers, each covered with a grubby white sheet. The doctor pulled the sheet over the nearest stretcher to one side. I was staring straight down into the face of a little girl, who could well have been just seven, as was claimed. She too had a gaping wound in her forehead where the bullet had struck her. It had exited at the right side of the back of her head, which was now just one bloody mess. The bullet had struck her with such force that her right eye was bulging and almost blown out of its socket looking like an over-dimensioned glass ball staring lifelessly into space. It was an appalling, horrific sight. My head was emptied of any rational thoughts but one. Again and again I heard myself saying, 'I can't believe it. It just can't be true!' I felt a desperate urge to leave the room but felt I had to stay and see the inspection through as agreed.

The three other victims were all men between 20 and 40, presumably soldiers. They, too, were killed by a single bullet. Two of them lay, like the little girl, with open eyes and they all had ashen grey faces. Rigor mortis had already set in, and it was only with difficulty that the doctor could show us the fatal bullet wounds. Unpleasant though it was to see these three dead men, it was the sight of the little girl that made the greatest impression. To shoot her with such cold-blooded ease was the most callous and inhuman deed I had ever encountered.

After the inspection, Oleg and I took our leave of Young Humo and returned home. Oleg poured two glasses of vodka which even by Russian standards were large. He told me that the sight of the little girl brought back all the memories of four years in Afghanistan like a bolt from the blue. He, too, was none too cheerful after what we had just seen. It was a seldom occurrence because normally I managed to maintain a professional distance from the suffering of the people, but this was an occasion on which my emotions got the better of me. I was seething with rage at the monster who had slaughtered that little girl and had to exercise supreme self-control at the ensuing meeting with the HVO liaison officer, where we reported what we had seen. Especially when they told us that she had been shot by Muslims in an attempt to put them in a poor light. We asked the HVO to report any similar instances of Armija BiH breaches of the most fundamental conventions for humane warfare. We received several reports to that effect but were never allowed to confirm them.

In the primitive environment of East Mostar, human contact assumed immense importance in maintaining normal human emotions. And after a day like this, our time with the family that evening was more valuable than ever. I think we all shuddered at the thought that their daughter, about the same age as the girl lying in that shed, could be the next victim to the innumerable snipers in Mostar, who seemed to be totally devoid of any kind of morality.

Oleg is a character worthy of a few words of description. With his round, somewhat featureless face and the endearing gap between his front teeth, he looked like an overgrown schoolboy and was often underestimated by those who did not know him. But beneath this bland exterior there was more than was apparent – much more. In critical situations he was amazingly calm, almost phlegmatic. Although he was both a good friend and colleague, despite many attempts it proved difficult to get to the heart of the man. It was almost as if he carried the burden of past experiences that he was unwilling to share with others. My natural curiosity, though, forced me to keep asking questions until I could find a reason for his secrecy. From the fragments of stories I had heard about Afghanistan I managed to piece together an incomplete picture of what he had done. He had learned the local language before being posted, and fought in Afghan uniform behind Afghan lines in a unit consisting solely of officers, a group which, incidentally, received considerably higher pay than the normal Russian officer. Oleg must have belonged to the special forces called *Spetsnaz* and undoubtedly carried around inside him vivid memories of tough and dirty operations that he no longer wanted to be confronted with.

Although there was little fun in Mostar, there are amusing incidents I look back on. One of them took place the day I paid a visit to the HQ of the Spanish battalion in Medugorje in one of our newly acquired vehicles, a Mitsubishi Pajero. I had parked within the confines of the camp and when I returned to the vehicle, I found a gaggle of Spanish soldiers gathered round it and slapping their thighs, convulsed with laughter. I tried to get out of them what was so amusing but none of them was capable of explanation. When I got back to the sector headquarters, however, Roberto let me in on the joke. With a loud guffaw he told me with great delight that *Pajero* was Spanish slang for a 'wanker' – a masturbating man.

Another funny incident, unlikely as it may seem, came from the front line in Mostar. Young Humo told us about it at one of our meetings. In the middle of the front line, not far from the Tito Bridge, there was a high school under HVO control. During a night patrol, two Armija BiH soldiers got so close to the building that in the first glimmerings of the dawn they could make out the profile of a man. They put their rifle stocks to their cheeks and fired. Nothing happened. They shot again. The man was still standing. Full of amazement, they called off their small action and scurried back to their unit to be de-briefed. As it was still not yet light, the Platoon Commander and Young Humo sneaked out into the semi-darkness to investigate. Shortly afterwards they returned, and half choking with laughter, were barely able to report that the man had indeed been hit, several times at that. The fact that he did not succumb and fall to the ground was because he was made of stone. It was a statue of one of Humo's ancestors.

On 18 June, there was not so much to laugh at, not as far as I was concerned anyway. Stan, the Dutchman who had relieved Oleg in the group rotation, and I had just concluded a meeting with our Croatian liaison officer and were on our way back to East Mostar. Since the shooting of the Spanish lieutenant, we had been very wary of using the Tito Bridge, which was normally by far the fastest route between the two parts of town. Some days earlier, the small victory was achieved of getting both parties to accept a ceasefire, to come into effect at 1200 on 18 June. When Stan and I got into our car outside HVO HQ, it was 1230 and the situation looked relatively peaceful. We discussed briefly whether we should take the bridge road or not. We decided we would.

It was four days since I had last crossed the bridge and as the entire area between it, the high school and the bank had been the centre of heavy fighting in the intervening days, I did not even know if the bridge was still standing. From the main street we drove along an avenue that came to an end where the real destruction began. We swung into the car park next to the bank and neared Racina Street, which we always drove cautiously down as it was a location where the two parties to the conflict always faced each other in stand-off position.

As we swung into the street the result of the last few days fighting became immediately apparent. The street was almost buried under a thick carpet of bricks and masonry and had become considerably narrower because of the houses that had collapsed. For a moment I thought we would never get past it all but the car kept bouncing its way onwards. Hardly had we managed to squeeze past the most forward Armija position, now expanded so that it almost filled the street, before my ears were deafened by a loud and high-pitched whining sound. At that moment I saw a small round hole in the windscreen, right between Stan and myself, and it occurred to me that we were under fire. He must have come to the same conclusion, because as I changed gear and revved the engine, I head him shout, 'Go, go, go!' Bang! The car took another hit, and another. I had no idea where the shots were coming from, so I took a chance and kept going at full speed in the direction we were heading. Bang! Bang! Bang! The incessant battering of the rounds hitting the car was literally deafening. I paid little attention to the fact that we had been hit and drove as if in a trance. I had only one thought in my head – we have to get out of here in a hurry. But there was still 80 metres to go . . . 70 . . . 60 . . . before I could turn off the street. All this time I could hear the bullets thumping into the car and never have I felt time stand quite so still. The car had become difficult enough to steer at low speed but by now we were going at quite a lick and it felt as if the car was being shaken from side to side and bounced up and down.

At last, we reached the end of the street and could turn away from that outlaw of a soldier that had adopted the practice of the lowest of the low and opened fire on an unarmoured, slow-moving, white UN vehicle. We were now going so fast a sharp swing to the left was out of the question, but I tried anyway. The result was that we continued directly towards the corner of a house on the opposite side of the street. Stan grabbed the dashboard and roared, 'Nooooo!' but in the same instant I regained control of the car. Even so, I managed to flatten a stop sign before we headed for the still intact Tito Bridge, fishtailing along the road. On the east bank of the Neretva, I took the first right and stopped the car. We sat still for a few seconds, staring first at the air in front of us and then at each other, with the same questioning expression – what the hell was that? When we discovered the rear of the car looked like a collander, we were almost ecstatic at our good luck. But the natural reaction soon set in and we were trembling from head to foot. And a little later, a feeling of intense anger swept over us.

Exactly how many shots were fired at us I do not know, but it is a fact that the rear end of the car was peppered with no less than 12 shots. One of them had punctured the right rear wheel, explaining why the car had been so difficult to steer. The spare wheel that was mounted on the tailgate was hit in three places and had it not been there, Stan would have had three bullets in the back. I escaped being shot in the head by only 20 cm by the first and most accurate shot that left the car through the front windscreen. I can still taste the bitterness we felt at being shot at by a soldier we had come here to help. The fact that the attack was made in single, individually aimed shots and not a burst of automatic fire made it even worse. I hope I never come to hate a person so much as I then hated that unknown soldier. There can be no doubt he was shooting to kill and that was pretty difficult to condone. The thought that he was still over there – alive – after he had almost put an end to us was almost unbearable and I felt furiously impotent. As it was, there was nothing I could do to him, but given the chance, there is no doubt what I would have done – and with a clean conscience at that.

When we had got over the initial shock, we went through the motions of changing the wheel so we could get back and make our report. But our arms were like jelly and we had to recruit local help to see us on our way. When we arrived safely at the house, we felt, not without reason, like two creatures spared by divine intervention, among the chosen few on this earth. As luck would have it, old Tehir had chosen that afternoon to give one of his party pieces from the *'gut'* old days. When we came up the drive with the car riddled with bullet-holes, the old man had taken position and was marching on the spot with his bandy legs and singing, in very broken German, a song from his days of glory. We paid him little attention and when he saw the car from behind, he understood why.

The same afternoon, Stan was picked up and taken to Medugorje before flying home to Holland for some leave. He was later to tell me that the sudden change in scenery had fallen well short of success. He had wandered around on a constant high, overstrung and unable to concentrate on what was going on around him. I remained in Mostar and the same evening the team and I celebrated the fact that I was still alive and kicking with two visiting British officers from the UN battalion in Zenica. We were all in good spirits, bordering on the riotous. Never had I felt so full of the joy of simply being alive after coming so perilously close to the alternative. In fact, I am not at all sure that what had happened had sunk in by that evening. I replayed the tapes in my head many times but the incident never, in any way, developed into actual trauma.

The shooting gave rise to a violent protest to the HVO, from whose side of the front line the shots undoubtedly came. It was the second time in a single week that the HVO had endangered the safety of a UN officer, with flagrant disregard for any existing agreement. As the Croats refused to accept any responsibility, our Senior Military Observer took drastic action and withdrew the entire team until sufficient guarantees for our safety had been provided from both sides. Strangely enough, the other members of the team and I were against this decision and believed it to be an over-reaction. We had got used to our working conditions and despite what had just happened, we had difficulty in accepting his viewpoint as reasonable. We felt very strongly that we still had unfinished business in this town. As it turned out, our 16 days in purgatory were over.

On 21 June, we lowered the large, blue UN flag which until then had marked the UN forward position on East Mostar. Team MX-5 was then 16 days old. Saying goodbye to my adopted family was a harrowing affair. Nedija cried her eyes out and everybody expected things to get even tougher and more unpleasant. They had regarded the UN flag and our presence as a guarantee for safety, unfortunately quite unjustifiably. It was wishful thinking. Our mandate was not respected and we could now well become a burden to the family.

We left East Mostar with a bad taste in our mouths and with the depressing feeling that we had failed in the moment of greatest need. As we drove away, the daily bouts of fighting were beginning to reappear. The ceasefire of 18 June had, of course, been broken long ago.

---

1. Pronounced 'Handchar', from the Turkish word for scimitar.
2. Representatives from the European Community Monitoring Mission (ECMM), as it was then known, who functioned as the Commission's eyes on the region. Their work was made difficult by the fact that the three warring parties regarded them as unimportant and would seldom give them the time of day. The Serbs often refused them permission to patrol as they regarded them as representatives from a German-dominated organisation.
3. The heliport a few kilometres south of Mostar was the base for some of the HVO forces in the town.
4. Nightvision is a large pair of binoculars with a light amplification system allowing the soldier to see up to about 1 km in the dark.

# Chapter 5

# Mostar – Constant Confrontation

T he first night at our digs in Medugorje was a sleepless one. There was a deathly hush. The air was as thick and still as treacle. I was lying there wondering what on earth it could be that was keeping me awake, when the obvious occurred to me. That was exactly the point – it was quiet. I had got used to the nocturnal pandemonium of battle and the silence seemed unnatural, threatening. The realisation was food for thought.

The episode of our shot-up car was a sensation. The Spanish crossed themselves and muttered *'Madre mia'* when they saw our moving collander. Stan and I looked upon it more as an old warhorse that had done its duty and now deserved to be put out to grass.

We felt a strange sadness as it was driven off to the large UN workshop in Zagreb, where it would probably be scrapped. It should have ended its days in a museum, but that was a decision in the hands of an MT (motor transport) sergeant who would doubtless take a less sentimental view of the twelve bullet-holes.

The report of the shooting and the team's subsequent evaluation caused the eyebrows of the UN senior officers in Kiseljak to disappear under their hats. On 21 June a fax ticked its way into our office. It was from Colonel Dijk, commander of all the Military Observers in Bosnia-Herzegovina. He congratulated Stan and I for our 'exemplary conduct', a recognition which awoke a sneaking feeling of both pride and happiness in me, despite the fact that our performance had an undoubted element of good fortune attached to it.

The HVO senior command received a blasting about the safety of the team, a broadside which obviously hit home. A few days later, our status and safety were guaranteed in a memorandum from General Petkovic, the Commanding General of the HVO, with the local commander, Lasic, co-signing the document. The promise was made that the contents of the memo would be communicated to all HVO units in Mostar. A similar guarantee had already been extended by the Armija BiH in Mostar, signed by Pasalic. All that was needed now to re-activate the team was permission from the UN in Kiseljak. On the afternoon of 25 June, it came.

In the four days from our enforced withdrawal to our renewed operational status, we had continued our daily patrols in both parts of town but had left before nightfall. Nor had we tempted fate by crossing the front line in the centre of town, apart from once and that was in a Spanish APC. We crossed instead either to the north via the dam or to the south via the Pilot Bridge. In the intervening period, we had begun to adapt to life outside Mostar and, for the first time, to think about our personal safety, something we had dismissed out of hand only a few days earlier. So it was with a spirit of pioneer adventure that, on the afternoon of 26 June, we set out for our base in East Mostar. The journey went without incident until we were stopped at an HVO check-point just to the east of the dam by a small, thin man with a manic, vacant expression on his face. As soon as he started speaking, he displayed a set of teeth half ravaged by decay.

'Please get out of the car so we can search it.'

His action was familiar and predictable, so I shoved under his nose our newly acquired guarantee of respect for our status and safety, signed by his commander-in-chief, the general in command of all HVO forces in Bosnia-Herzegovina. His reaction, however, was far from predictable. When he had read the official document, he nonchalantly tossed it onto the floor of the car with a contemptuous snort and informed us that in these parts, he was in charge.

'I don't believe my eyes,' muttered Rob, with a look of dumb-founded amazement on his face, staring first at me and then at the piece of paper on the floor. The little runt of a soldier repeated his arrogant demand, 'Search or stay where you are'.

We tried to show him the letter again – this time he disdained even reading it. We were left with no alternative but to turn back, impotent in the knowledge that our auspicious guarantee had not a fraction of the value we had believed and accepted in good faith. Things had taken a turn for the worse.

The next morning, Rob and I drove to Mostar yet again, but this time straight to HVO Military Police HQ to be given an explanation for the remarkable incident of the previous day. To make sure there were no misunderstandings, we took our interpreter with us. We were welcomed by the duty officer, whose fine features, well-groomed hair and round granny glasses made him look more like a student from a past era than an army captain in the middle of a dirty war. I told him what had happened, explained the formal agreements that existed and finally showed him our written 'guarantee'. We should have saved our energy. He had never seen nor heard of this document and could not care less. All he wanted to talk about was gun running for the Armija BiH. Discussion was obviously fruitless and I changed tack and explained the purpose and practicalities of our mission and the importance of our neutrality. It seemed to do the trick – this was information he could handle and before long he had promised to call the check-point in question and give orders for our free passage.

The atmosphere became a little less icy now and I allowed myself to drop a remark about a large photograph hanging on the wall above his desk. It was a portrait of Ante Pavelic[1]. 'I see old Ante has found new honour and dignity,' I said.

The captain, who clearly did not believe I had the faintest idea who Ante Pavelic was, tried to dismiss the observation with a tense shrug of his shoulders and a doubtful tale about inheriting the office inventory from his predecessor. On my way out, I saw that his was not the only office so equipped. The parallel with senior officers in German police stations bedecking their walls with pictures of Hitler was inescapable.

We left the HQ with an uncomfortable feeling that what we had just witnessed was evidence of a total lack of military discipline. It was unimaginable that a captain in the HVO should display such utter disregard for a letter from his commander-in-chief. But so it was, and the similar reaction from the little guard the day before was now explained with horrifying clarity. This blinding realisation recalled all the other incidents and led us to the inevitable conclusion that Mostar was a nest of outlaw warriors – people fighting their own personal vendettas in blissful independence of the agreements reached by the superiors who were running the war. If this were true, it was no longer difficult to understand how Stan and I were shot at and the Spanish lieutenant killed.

The family in our old lodgings were delighted with our reunion and not many minutes had passed before Nedija was standing at the door saying *'kaaffa'*, her un-butlerish but clearly intelligible way of telling us coffee was served downstairs. But our domestic pleasure was short-lived. Hardly had we sat down before a concerto of loud bangs on the outer walls of the house started up. A quick peek through the crack of the door revealed that the house had been hit by a salvo from a light machine-gun. So much for the untouchability of the white car parked outside, which the gunman could not have failed to see. (Or perhaps that is what made him pull the trigger?) It boded ill but to remove the last vestiges of doubt of our identity, we hurriedly hoisted the blue flag of the UN over the building. Team MX-5 was back in business.

We passed the early evening in the bosom of the family but at 2030, I made my apologies and went to my room to write up my diary. At 2050 precisely, just as I was describing the events of the day, there was a burst of deafening explosions around the house. I threw myself to the floor and tiger-crawled to a wall that provided some meagre protection. RATATATATA – another salvo, and another. The luminescent green lines of tracer they were using showed it was coming from the west. I got on the radio to Medugorje.

'Mike X-ray,' (the call-sign of our HQ) 'this is Mike X-ray 5. We are under fire!'

'Say again Mike X-ray 5. You are very broken up.'

'I say again. Shooting for God's sake. We're under fire. Call the HVO and get them to bloody stop!'

I crawled over to the field telephone to call HVO HQ myself in the desperate hope that I might be able to talk to an English-speaking officer. I was in luck and I wasted no time in giving the man an earful of what his troops were doing. Another salvo hit the ground in front of the house. And another, and another and another. Ten in all. Suddenly all was quiet and I waited anxiously to see how long it would last. Rob came bursting through the door from the stairwell, his face wild with excitement and apprehension. He had been sitting in the driver's seat of our car when the first salvo shrieked past, two metres over the roof, and tore into the hillside. He had taken cover behind the family's woodpile, where he found old Tehir also sheltering.

At 2110, the field telephone gave its shrill call. It was the duty officer at the HVO HQ informing us that 'the commanding officer has given orders to cease fire immediately'. Well, that's nice of him, I thought. Rob and I went outside to see what damage had been done and saw that several immediate neighbours had had their walls redecorated by the salvos from the anti-aircraft cannon. Our house had only received a few direct hits at ground level, though the ground around the house was effectively ploughed up. A weapon such as this is highly accurate at that range, so it was clear that their intention had not been to kill us. That would have been child's play. But the message to us from the HVO was plain and unambiguous – GET OUT!

By now, I was sick and tired of the HVO campaign of dirty tricks and when, an hour later, a mortar shell landed so close to the house that the walls shook and plaster cascaded down from the ceiling, it was the last straw. This was raving insanity. Rob agreed. We called the SMO over the radio and asked him seriously to consider another shut-down of our observation post because as far as relations between the Croats and the UNMOs were concerned, we had reached a state of constant confrontation. The next morning, he came over to the house for a more detailed report of what had happened. But he was reluctant to pull us out, even though it was at the team's instigation this time and not his. I think he was worried about losing face with UN chiefs in Kiseljak. The dilemma between his pride and our skins upset us more than a little. As brave and decisive as he had been a week earlier in withdrawing us at his own discretion, it was beyond our understanding that he could hesitate now, when all the official guarantees for our safety had proved to be as useful as a fire extinguisher in hell.

He would, however, accept a temporary relocation to Medugorje until we could find a less vulnerable base. That was hardly the main issue but we decided to hold fire on the broadside we wanted to blast him with. The priority task was to pack up all our kit and say goodbye, again, to the family. It was no easier this time to take our leave of these people who had done so much for us and showed us so much kindness. It was not all in vain. We had, at least, established once and for all that we were like a red rag to a bull for the HVO troops and as difficult as it was to convince Nedija, the family would be better off without us. Striking our flag was a decidedly unpleasant job. It had been stretched with ropes attached to all four corners and these had to be untied and stowed before the flag could come down. The heavy heart with which I fumbled with our knots, terribly exposed to the whims of the local snipers, whom we now knew beyond doubt had not the shadow of respect for our status, will be with me forever. Never before had I felt so vulnerable and humiliated and I hope I never shall again. It was also the only occasion in my time in former Yugoslavia when I really felt the bite of fear in my entrails.

The next two days were spent trying to find a new home for our base, with the cooperation of the Armija BiH command, but with the shortage of accommodation in the eastern part of town, it was no easy task. Our Croatian liaison officer advised us, with the best of intentions to be fair, not to move to East Mostar, giving us a veiled confirmation that there were indeed HVO units there that were less than delighted with our presence and which operated outside the military chain of command.

On the morning of 30 June, a Norwegian colleague and I were stopped 5 km from Mostar on the Medugorje road at a checkpoint that was normally unmanned. It was now crammed with military policemen who were armed to the teeth. Land-mines had been laid across both traffic lanes and access to the town effectively denied. We were speechless when we learned what was going on. To everyone's surprise, the Armija BiH had attacked the HVO early that morning from many sides and taken the Tihomer Mesic barracks in the northern part of town. A narrow corridor had also been established from the north of town to the Armija BiH forces in central Bosnia.

It struck us all as a Herculean achievement, particularly considering the desperate plight of the Muslims. But then, perhaps, with their backs to the wall they had found hidden reserves of strength and determination to break out of the iron grip that had held them in check. But the fact that it was possible at all is due chiefly to poor Croatian management of the defence of West Mostar, perhaps excused by the fact that until then, the Muslims had been overpowered into adopting a purely defensive posture. Whatever scenarios the strategic analysts could come up with, the Armija BiH attack had brought down an iron curtain between Mostar and Medugorje and until further notice there was no way for us to get into the town. Amazingly, Lasic, chief of the HVO in Mostar, gave UNPROFOR the blame for his own inadequate leadership. Such accusations from a senior officer were nothing short of pathetic.

For the next 14 days, we set out each day to try and discover an open road into town. From time to time, they clipped our wings further by restricting our mobility to Medugorje and effectively putting us under 'town arrest'. At these times, we could only follow the situation from the newspapers, the people of Medugorje and the Spanish UN battalion, who kept their ear close to the ground among the locals. That is rather a coy way of putting it – they had informers, probably paid by themselves, in Mostar (perhaps in both HVO and Armija BiH). We soon learned that Hujdur, commander of the brigade in which Esad Humo was next in command, had been killed in the 30 June offensive.

One day after being turned back at Mostar and returning home to Medugorje, a colleague and I were stopped by a gaggle of women. There must have been about 40 of them, shouting and waving their arms madly for us to stop. They were all Muslims who lived in HVO-controlled territory south of Mostar. For fear that the Armija BiH push would continue south towards the coastal town of Neum, the HVO had interned their husbands to prevent them joining forces with Armija BiH units. They had been taken to a concentration camp. The woman were begging and pleading for us to take them there to see how their men were being treated. 'Help us! Please help us!' they chanted, with tears streaming down their cheeks. But with us barred from Mostar, this was definitely a job for the Red Cross, to whom we wasted no time in passing on the request.

On 8 July, our HQ was contacted by a captain from the British battalion at Zenica. He was one of the pair that had visited the Mostar team on the evening of 18 June and had just been called from one of the Armija BiH's very few working phones that up to then had been a well-kept secret. Esad Humo had made an emotional appeal for UNPROFOR's assistance in evacuating his brother. Young Humo had received serious head wounds and lay unconscious and attached to a respirator in the East Mostar hospital. Had this situation arisen before the Armija BiH attack of 30 June, evacuation would have been possible through the HVO lines but any form of humanitarian help was now impossible. Esad Humo knew this very well and was trying to win UN support to have his brother evacuated through Serbian lines. We tried to arrange something through our teams on the Serbian side of the front line but there was little we could do.

Over the next few days, we were helpless spectators to Humo's desperate struggle to help his young brother, who was growing weaker by the hour. He left no stone unturned and pulled strings with his pre-war contacts in both Serbian and Croatian camps. A few days later, on 12 July, Young Humo died after being in a coma for five days. His death affected all of us who had worked in the Mostar team. We had got to know him and respect him as a bright young man with a giant and bubbling personality. He was 28, trained as a civil engineer and would undoubtedly have achieved a prominent position in his country if he had survived the war.

In mid-July, I took 14 days leave at the Croatian coast. It had been three months since I had had my last day off and it was a break I very much needed. When I was picked up at Split two weeks later, everything had changed. I had been assigned to another sector and was to report as soon as possible to the UN observers in Zadar, halfway up the coast.

I left Bosnia-Herzegovina with memories for life – good and bad. I had seen indescribable destruction and human suffering. But I had also enjoyed the immense comradeship with the other observers and experienced immeasurable human kindness and hospitality.

I felt indifferent to all the opponents in the political arena but a great deal of heartfelt sympathy for the ordinary people whom I had seen at close hand, fighting bravely for their lives and existence.

Understandably, my impressions of the HVO were far from positive. I learned later from colleagues that in other places in Bosnia-Herzegovina the HVO were more amenable. In Mostar, the opposite was true, from generals to private soldiers and at every link in the chain and every organisation in the army.

The war between the Croats and Muslims continued with unabated ferocity until March 1994, when an American initiative brought peace between them. No great changes had been seen in the Mostar sector since I had left it. A new federation had been created with the alliance between the Muslims and the Croats, and the partners who had been at each others throats shortly before were now firm allies against the Bosnian Serbs. Behind this lies Balkan logic at its most demonstrative and an interesting bit of politics whose details are unknown to me.

The family in East Mostar survived the Croat-Muslim war. All except old Tehir who fell to a sniper in early November 1993, as he stood puffing on one of his roll-your-owns. He was found by his grandchildren in the drive of their house. He had come through two wars as a front line soldier with nothing but scratches and bruises. But the war in Mostar, raging just beyond his garden path, was his Waterloo. Such is fate.

> I will turn grey one day, and old but
> My Mostar will ever be my maid
> I will turn grey one day, and old but
> My Mostar will never age or fade.[2]

1. During World War II, Ante Pavelic was the leader of the Croatian fascists, the *Ustashe.* See footnotes in chapter 1.
2. Refrain from the melancholy folk song, *Moj Mostar* (My Mostar) from before the Croat-Muslim war. Written by Dino Dervishalidovic.

## Chapter 6

# Sibenik – Paradise Found

T he road from Split to Zadar runs along the Adriatic coast, where steep cliffs and crystal, azure water had a magnetic attraction for tourists in their thousands before the war. However except for a very few adventurers and other hardy souls, they had all fled and the economy of the entire region was suffering badly as a result. The myriad hotels and restaurants were fighting a price war as fierce as the hot war being waged elsewhere in the country and prices were at rock bottom. But although the Croatian riviera, known as Dalmatia, was in economic difficulties, it was considerably more wealthy and developed than the region I had come from in Bosnia-Herzegovina. Millionaire villas were no unusual sight in this playboy belt and the marinas were packed with expensive yachts.

In UN jargon, the area I was to work in now was known as Sector South and comprised the southern part of Croatia from Gospić, north of Zadar, to Sinj, east of Split. (See the map section.) The territory in Sector South was bisected from north to south by a front line. This division separated the Croats from the Krajinan Serbs who had occupied the area since the autumn of 1991 and expelled virtually all Croats. The area now under the control of *Hrvatska Vojska* (HV), the Croatian Army, varied in width from 2 to 40 kilometres, widest in the north, tapering to a minimum just east of Zadar. With a very few exceptions, the front line had remained unchanged since new year 1991/92, since when the war between Croats and Serbs had been waged with long-range artillery.

The situation in Croatia was problematic though far less chaotic than in Bosnia-Herzegovina. The current front line was not the same as that settled on in the drafting of UNPROFOR's mandate. In the intervening period between the ratification of the mandate and the deployment of UN troops, local Serbs had taken another patch of land along the border to Bosnia-Herzegovina, still known by its old name, Krajina[1]. The local Serbs refused to leave the enclaves they had occupied, which created a problem for UNPROFOR, as the areas lay outside its mandate. The solution was found in both parties agreeing that UN observers – and only them – could patrol these areas which we called Pink Zones.

On 22 January, 1993 the Croatian Army reconquered a few areas of territory. Only a few – but they were of crucial importance to the Krajinan Serbs and the Croats were adamant in their refusals to withdraw. The Croatian government had made the Serbs an offer that guaranteed certain sovereignty rights, including considerable autonomy within a Croatian state. Bearing in mind that Krajina is, and always has been, part of Croatia, the agreement was attractive, even to many of the local Serbs. The real problem at this time was that the Serbs did not trust the Croats as far as they could spit and feared reprisals from the moment they laid down their arms. The Croatian proposal was therefore rejected out of hand.

This was the situation when I arrived in the area on that gorgeous summer day in 1993.

The reason why I and many other UNMOs had had to move to Sector South in such a hurry was that the UN command hoped that a breakthrough in the stalled peace process would at last be achieved. The Croatian government had accepted that the army would pull out of those areas it had regained in January of the same year. They would then be demilitarised and put under UNPROFOR protection. They were now classified as Blue Zones. The UN hoped they would become the key to the solution of the entire Croatian problem and every effort was made to ensure success.

The most important Blue Zone was the area around the Maslenica Bridge east of Zadar. In the winter months, the bridge was the only safe lifeline between north and south Dalmatia. The area around Zemunik Airport was also important for the maintenance of a viable and working infrastructure. Both were in Zadar team territory. I was to reinforce the Sibenik team some 75 km south of Zadar. Here it was the Milevahic plateau, 15 kilometres square of dusty and barren terrain, that was a Blue Zone. This area was different in that it had been reconquered in June 1992. Negotiations were proceeding extremely slowly, accusations and counter-accusations were hurled back and forth between the two parties. The UN made great efforts to make possible the implementation of the plan but it was almost as if neither party ever really entered wholeheartedly into the spirit of things. After a few weeks, the whole plan fell apart and the UNMO reinforcements were returned to their sectors.

The time had arrived for a change of sector anyway and I and a few others were ordered to stay where we were.

Life here on the Croatian coast was very different from that I had led in Bosnia-Herzegovina. The team consisted of seven officers from five different countries and lived with a wonderful Croatian family of three generations in an idyllic little village called Brodarica, a few kilometres south of Sibenik. It was sheer paradise. The shelves in the shops were full and we were free from worrying about food, washing up, laundry or any other practical chores. Our relationship with our host family was excellent and before long, all of us had fallen for the family's 2½-year-old daughter, Ivana. When we were not out on patrol we spent much of our time diving and fishing with Dane, the son of the family. Fresh oysters were daily fare. Our closest neighbour was the sea and our constant companion, the sun. The final touch to the picture of almost impossible fantasy was that not a single shell had fallen in Brodarica. I felt as if I had passed through the gates to Paradise Found.

Fighting in the Sibenik sector was intermittent and limited to sporadic bursts of fire each day from one side of the front line to the other, with the occasional flare-up that embraced towns and villages on both sides of the front line. But at Zadar, things were very different. Here both Maslenica Bridge and Zemunik Airport were heavily bombarded. Zadar itself was not spared and nor were the towns on the Serbian side of the front line.

The low intensity of fighting meant that casualties were few and far between, which contributed to an atmosphere that was much less tense than in Bosnia-Herzegovina. Understandably enough, the Croats were highly frustrated that they were still unable to return to their homes, a promise firmly given in the UN resolutions. Generally speaking, they felt bitter towards the UN but here in the Sibenik area, they never allowed their anger to grow into concrete threats. Their way of the demonstrating their rage was much more suppressed. A single incident serves as a good example. A group of private soldiers from the HV had taken up position on the side of the road on one of our patrol routes.

They had written in large letters on a piece of cardboard, '*Samo Sloga Srbina Spasava*[2] = UN' and underneath, 'Boutros Gahli = *Cetnik*[3]'.

The entire incident was undramatic and when it dawned on the soldiers that we were at a level of the UN hierarchy that could do nothing about their problems they had an attack of bad conscience and invited us to a meal and *slivovic*. This episode serves as a vivid illustration of the relationship between the Croats and ourselves in the Sibenik area. Most of them did not like us much for what we represented but treated us pretty well as people.

The relationship with the HV high command was marked by a tone of friendliness but was otherwise completely unproductive. Our mobility was much more controlled and monitored than it had been in Mostar. We were, for example, strictly forbidden to visit the front line without the escort of a Croatian liaison officer and very few of our requests for patrols were granted, with the result that we saw little of the units we really wanted to see. Instead, our time was spent on one hilltop after another, kilometres from the front line. It felt like playing tourist and after a couple of weeks I was bored out of my skull. Life was wonderful – too wonderful. I had come here to do a job, not to get a suntan. Quite simply, the HV did not want us driving around from one front line unit to another, officially because the reality of the situation was the ceasefire we were there to enforce did not exist. This being the case, we found it very difficult to understand what the hell we were doing there at all. The execution of this 'hold-us-at-bay' strategy was implemented by our three liaison officers, who took it in turns to shadow us everywhere we went. Despite our conflicting interests, we enjoyed a good relationship with this trio, each of whom was very different and each of whom had a touch of originality about them. They had differing opinions about the war and represented three different life styles, which made them interesting company to keep. During the patrols, they were always with us in our car and topics of conversation and exchanges of views depended on which one of them was on duty.

One of them, Milivoje, was 40 years old but could easily have passed for somebody five or ten years younger. Before the war, he was a guide at a local hotel complex known as Solaris. He was a confirmed bachelor and such a job offered him ample opportunity to indulge in his favourite sporting activity – womanising. Despite the fact that he had been doing this for the best part of 20 years, there were no signs that he was about to go off the boil in any way. From the moment he closed the car door behind him until he opened it again at the end of a patrol he chattered incessantly about women. Blessed with the gift of the humorous raconteur, his performance was more entertaining than wearing. Women were never referred to as other than 'good material' and he wished ardently for peace so he could return to the Don Juan life he used to lead in those lazy, hazy days at Solaris. His views on the conflict were flamboyantly prag-matic without the slightest trace of ideology. He was prepared to enter peace agreements with anybody and if they would leave him alone, he would return the compliment. He was about as unmilitary as it is possible to be. He was not one to take chances and was so intent on finding safety and security he could have been accused of being a wimp. I firmly believe he will meet his end at the ripe old age of 85, still happily engaging in his favourite pastime.

His absolute opposite was Tony, a 27-year-old Croatian Canadian, who before the war had been a test driver for Chrysler in Canada. He had joined up as a volunteer when the war broke out and never tried to hide the fact that he thoroughly enjoyed the hectic months around the end of 1991 and the beginning of 1992 when he fought with the newly-formed Croatian army against the JNA. I am not saying that he preferred war to peace but he did not regard it as a personal disaster to be in the thick of the fighting. In fact, he got a kick out of it. The land that had been lost worried him greatly. He was one of those who would never accept anything short of the full and complete return of Krajina to Croatian hands. The alternative was far worse than an extension of hostilities. He was a straightfor-ward, non-academic man of action, without in any way bearing the stigma of stupidity or ignorance. He too had a ready quip for each woman we saw on our patrols, comments totally unsuitable for repetition for those with a nervous disposition. He was the closest thing I have seen to the Action Man toys I had as a boy and I will bet a king's ransom that as a child he was constantly put into deten-tion after school for such horrendous crimes as pulling pigtails and tying shoe laces together. Assuming for a moment that he ever went to school.

The last member of the trio was 27-year-old Ivo, who had the sharpest brain of the three, without any doubt. He had a degree in English and his whole bearing and behaviour bore the mark of acad-emia, perhaps even with a touch of arrogance but an arrogance that seemed natural somehow. His spoken English was delivered with such grammatical exactitude and immaculate pronunciation that even the British officers were impressed. He loved every moment of the praise heaped upon him and blatantly encouraged it. His utterly correct comments on Tony's cavalier descriptions of women were priceless, assuming of course that you could appreciate the contrasts between the two individuals. For him, the war was nothing other than his life being put on hold. But he did regard it as an essential, if primitive, means of regaining the land his country had lost, a demand which he would not under any circumstances relinquish. He used to talk of a girlfriend but I am not convinced, if the truth be told, he would not rather curl up with a good book.

Because our patrols were, of necessity, quite short at this time, I had more than enough time to write up my diary. One afternoon went to recording the stories I had heard from other UNMOs who had come close to a premature ending of their careers – and lives. The list ended up far longer than I reckoned and reading the numerous accounts of other UNMOs who had emerged unscathed from hairy situations engendered in me a fatalistic attitude towards this period of my life. Once more I speculated on the unpredictability of fate. Some people are unlucky enough to cross the road and get run over, whilst others survive the most grotesque situations. Just read this:

Sarajevo, autumn 1992. A UNMO team is gathered in the living room of their house on the Muslim side of the front line, right in the middle of Sarajevo. Mortar shells are falling all around, many uncomfortably close to the house. Suddenly, there is a loud crash and the coffee table collapses. They look down in horror to see that a mortar shell has penetrated the roof and buried itself in the floor without detonating. Had this shell not been a dud, five UNMOs would have been posted on the 'killed in action' lists at UNPROFOR HQ.

Central Bosnia, summer 1993. A Spanish major new to the Sector was on his first patrol. He and his partner were forced to stop at an unmanned road block consisting of a number of anti-tank mines piled on top of each other. Hardly had they drawn to a halt before the Spanish major received a blow to the head which knocked him unconscious. His partner managed to get them to safety and discovered that a rifle bullet had penetrated his friend's kevlar helmet just over his temple. What had saved his life was that the bullet had first passed through the metal window frame a few centimetres from his head.

Gorazde, June 1993. The observer to take the record for the closest of shaves must be the Norwegian captain who was hit by four 12.7-mm sniper bullets during a patrol in the Gorazde pocket. Two of the bullets hit his armoured breastplate, one hit him in the side and the last punctured a lung and nicked his heart. Six hours passed between the attack and his receiving any form of treatment. The doctor who performed the surgery said he had been one hour and one millimetre from death. He recovered fully.

It was episodes such as these that generated the oft-heard epithet, 'God is a UNMO'.

Life for the Zadar team was to hot up. In early August, two UNMOs were patrolling the Maslenica Bridge, which had been going through an unfortunate cycle of being bombed by the Serbs and repaired by the Croats. They were standing on the approaches to the bridge when it came under heavy artillery fire. The UNMOs managed to reach shelter behind a wall of sandbags but their car was blown to pieces. Zadar itself came under almost daily attack. Things were very different for us here in Sibenik, which slept as Zadar burned.

On 22 August, the town of Vodice, 10 km north-west of Sibenik, became the next victim of the terror attacks on towns that were made by both sides. Throughout the day, there had been a gradual escalation of hostilities and Vodice came under direct attack at about 1600, when the town centre was hit by some ten 128-mm rockets, each 2.8 metres long. Together with Simon from Kenya, I drove off to confirm the HV report. With us was Tony, one of the Three Musketeer liaison officers. We drove with an escort of the local police, which, as it turns out, was a good thing. We arrived an hour after that attack, so the shell holes were still smoking. At our first stop, the rocket had landed ten metres from a house, caused minor damage and set fire to the trees in the garden. The family had been at the beach during that attack, and there were no casualties. Reaction among the locals varied greatly. The owners of the house were very kind to us and even invited us to *slivovic*. Others were extremely bristly and hostile. One man swore and cursed in Serbo-Croatian, but we got the gist what of he was saying and were in no doubt that his slander was addressed to us. Another came slowly up to us and suddenly bent down to pick up a stone which the police barely managed to prevent him throwing at us. Anger and frustration was oozing out of many of the people around us and we, the representatives of international law and order, were prime targets for the release of their pent-up aggression. It was an educational, if unpleasant, experience.

Another rocket had fallen a metre from a house and blown off an entire corner, leaving the contents of the room behind the wall pouring into the street. When the rocket hit, the family had been eating their supper in the next room.

By a miracle, nobody in the town was hurt by the attack, even though all six rockets that we could confirm had fallen close to private homes. Vodice had no military targets worth speaking of, so what we were seeing was a purely terrorist attack. Regrettably, there were many such attacks in Sector South.

On August 29, our team was requested to send a UNMO to reinforce the team in Zadar, which was under great pressure as a result of the almost frenzied activity. I volunteered. Brodarica was beautiful and Sibenik a haven of peace, but I had already had enough of our pointless patrols and looked forward to taking my leave, saddened only by saying goodbye to good comrades and our wonderful surrogate family.

1. The full name of the area was *Vojna granica Krajina* – the military border of Krajina. It was established by Austria in 1578 and consisted of a belt of land that was to act as a buffer zone against the Ottoman empire. Expelled Serbs were allowed to settle here in exchange for their services as frontier guards. The area soon acquired a sizeable Serbian population which, down the generations, put down deep roots and developed its own identity, with military pride as one of its pillars.
2. 'Unity alone will save the Serbs', an old and much-flaunted Serbian slogan. The sentence was accompanied by a sort of logo consisting of a cross with four Cs back to back in each corner of the cross. This badge was posted throughout the Serb-controlled area in Croatia and Bosnia-Herzegovina.
3. Boutros Gahli was the Secretary General of the UN. See previous footnote 6 on 'Cetnik' in Chapter 3.

## Chapter 7

# Zadar – Learning to Love the Shriek of the Shells

After a brief spell of leave, I headed for Zadar on 9 September. Zadar is a coastal town with a very old city centre engulfed by modern buildings, often in concrete and often high-rise. The modern quarter is criss-crossed by long, broad avenues and the overall impression the town gives is one of size rather than charm. This was the fifth time in five months I had struck camp, the usual lot of a UNMO. And it suited me fine. It was 1100 when I turned off the main road for the town centre, with old Johann Sebastian belting out his intricate and immaculate perfection. There was a lot of traffic but the streets were deserted. There was not a living soul to be seen.

Driving in this traffic was like being in the chariot race in *Ben Hur* – people drove like maniacs, including the two ambulance drivers who suddenly bah-booed their way past me. The Hotel Kolovara, home of the UNMO office in the heart of the town, on the other hand was packed with people – frightened people. I knew there was something dreadfully wrong but it still came as a shock to hear that only minutes before I arrived, the town centre – and the hotel – had come under attack by artillery and battle tanks. Just two minutes before I got out of my car, an office block barely 200 metres from the hotel had been hit by a shell. If the gunlayer in that tank had elevated his barrel a few degrees higher, the shell would have passed over the office block and ploughed into the end of the hotel that housed the UNMO office. It was quite a welcome and I learned never to play music loud when driving in town, an unwritten rule we otherwise followed religiously when near the front line.

Our Croatian liaison officer, who had an office on the other side of the corridor from ours, soon let us know that the attack had cost at least one life. When it looked as though the attack was over, for now at least, a British UNMO, David, and I were dispatched to confirm this information. We did not need to go far. The victim was in the office block next door to the hotel. Rumours of the fatality had already spread to the hotel guests, mostly Croatian refugees from Krajina, and we were met by a wall of silent people. They did not need to speak, their faces and body language said it all in sullen silence: 'Stop this war! In God's name, why don't you stop this war?!' I understood their anger, sympathised with their situation. But I could not for the life of me fathom that so many people could harbour such great and unrealistic expectations of a handful of unarmed UN observers.

The office block had been hit at first floor level by a shell with a delayed action fuse. The entire floor, about 15 offices, was completely destroyed. Glass splinters, paper, chunks of woodwork, bookshelves and furniture lay higgledy-piggledy like a handful of scattered Pick Sticks. Everything was shattered, even the partition walls between the offices were rent in twain. In the office closest to the explosion, there was the body of a middle-aged man, killed instantly and now half buried in office equipment. His face was a grotesque mask of congealing blood. His hair was white and dusty from the plaster on the ceiling and walls. The other people who worked in that office had just gone for lunch when the shell hit. Many of them now stood frozen in horror at the thought that only minutes before the inferno broke loose they had been sitting a few metres from the poor man who had died such a violent death.

Our next call was to the yacht harbour, where a shell had fallen in the grass verge between two traffic lanes. Three cars had been parked where the shell had made its impact. They were all blown to smithereens. A family of three had been sitting in one car. Miraculously, the parents escaped, shocked to the core, with only minor cuts and bruises but their ten-year-old son had been seriously injured and now lay in a coma at the town hospital. The doctors thought it unlikely that he would recover. Both the office block and yacht harbour were about 10 km from the nearest military target. Once again, this was a purely terrorist attack.

We conducted these sorties with a peculiar prickling sensation in the back of our necks. We would have been inhuman if we had been able to dismiss totally the thought that another shell may, at that very moment, be entering the breech block, ready for firing at the same target. It was this sneaking feeling of 'the next one may have your name on it' and the human tragedies we had witnessed that made investigating these terrorist bombardments such a strain on the nerves.

Back at the UNMO office, I met my new colleagues for the first time – a motley crew from practically all over the world. At fifteen men strong, we were much larger than a normal team and rather immodestly nicknamed ourselves, 'Sector Zadar'. Team leader was Peter Halgunset from Norway, a beefy 35-year-old chewer of snuff with the blue eyes and blond hair that fully met up to the team's expectations of a Scandinavia inhabited by large and muscular marauding Vikings. Peter had been in Srebrenica in March 1993 when General Marillon had stormed into the area and proclaimed to the terrified residents, 'You are now under the protection of the UN forces'. Peter said that he had never seen anything so chaotic in his life. Another larger than life character in the team was Peter's deputy, John, a fiery Canadian officer whose bandy legs gave away the fact he was from a cavalry regiment. He spoke a direct, almost brutal, North American English, liberally peppered with well-tried and trusted Anglo-Saxon delicacies such as 'fuck', 'shit' and 'fucking' forming the basic ingredients in a rich recipe. To us, he was never known as anything but 'Fucking John'. After being introduced to the rest of the team David and I drove off to the OP (observation post) at the Maslenica Bridge, where we were to spend the next two days.

The area around the bridge had once been a combat zone, as the many ruined buildings revealed. There had been fierce fighting on two occasions – once when the Krajinan Serbs had taken the area and again, a year later in January 1993, when the Croats repossessed it. As explained earlier, in the winter the bridge was the only reliable link between north and south Dalmatia. Almost one million Croatians lived south of the bridge, which made it of enormous importance. For this reason, it was virtually a demand that the UN provide corroborative information when the Serbs launched an attack on it and cut the lifeline of those one million people. Just to put this in true perspective, let it not be forgotten that, officially at least, a ceasefire was in force, though the casual and untrained observer could be forgiven for thinking otherwise.

The original Maslenica Bridge had been blown up in the first few months of the war and a pontoon bridge erected some 700 metres away. The terrain around the bridge was barren and stony with steep cliff faces that fell to the cobalt blue water. The OP was sited on the top of a cliff, about 100m above sea level and 800m from the pontoon bridge. From here, we had a panoramic view that allowed us to observe Serbian tanks, some six or seven kilometres away. They had a free range to the bridge – and for that matter, to the OP as well. Apart from the tanks, the Serbs had two artillery positions 7 and 13 kilometres distant. We could not see these gun emplacements but our colleagues on the Serbian side of the line told us that it was from here the fire on the bridge invariably came.

To defend the bridge, the Croats had a couple of anti-aircraft guns and an infantry unit of indeterminate size 500m from the OP and 300m from the bridge's eastern approach road. They also had an artillery position 500m behind us to the north. The Serbs took regular pot shots at the bridge, the A-A guns and the artillery position, so although the OP was in a perfect position for the work we had to do, it was not the most comfortable of places when all hell broke loose. Normally, however, Serbian fire was so accurate that shells never fell closer than 100m from the OP, so things were never as dangerous as they seemed when the fireworks display started. Only the previous week, the Croats had had the bright idea of using the OP as a shield and started constructing a bridge span on the large car park right next door to us. The UNMOs tried to persuade them to move it but to no avail. So they attempted to abandon ship and evacuate the OP – again with no luck – a road block had been put up. The Serbs had seen what was going on and before long shells began falling on the car park. Jamal from Jordan, one of the two unlucky UNMOs on duty at the time, told me later he had thought his last hour had come when he was sitting in the makeshift shelter, being showered with plaster from a ceiling that was springing cracks under the pressure of the ear-splitting explosions. The team complained vehemently to the HV over the flagrant abuse of our status. They promised just as vehemently that it would not happen again. But could we trust them?

The OP was located in what used to be a restaurant which before the war must have been a lucrative business. The surroundings, at any rate, were perfect. The building offered views of the sea and the mountains and was the ideal place to admire a sunrise or sunset. Paradise. But as it stood now, it was hardly the place for a romantic candlelight dinner. It had taken more than its fair share of direct hits, thankfully before the UNMOs moved in. The most visible of these battle scars was a large round hole in the building's façade, the result of a tank shell which had also split the interior wall completely. Nobody had found the time nor energy to make good the damage, so all the shattered contents hung from the walls like entrails and lay in random piles on the floor. Perhaps the most unsavoury reason for its unsuitability for a seductive supper was that when the Serbs had occupied it, they had used the entire building as a lavatory. When the UNMOs commandeered the building, thirty HV soldiers were ordered to clean it up and remove the enemy's piles of excrement and other human remains which lay everywhere in abundant deposits. They had not tackled this unenviable task with equal enthusiasm in every room. In many places I could still see the evidence of dried human faeces, which the local brown rats found irresistible. They were large creatures that scurried around the whole building – on one occasion, I even saw one in our bedroom. These were the conditions under which we had to live, sleep and eat for two days at a time. Having wrinkled my nose and shaken my head at this unspeakable disgusting mess, I found I could accept the situation surprisingly well and was amazed once more at what people can adapt to if there is no alternative.

When we were not actively observing from the converted terrace, our main recreation room was a $2 \times 6$m room that served as dining room, sitting room and bedroom. The only furniture was two iron beds, literally on their last legs, with springs as soft as perished elastic, and a small table on which we could store our food supplies and which presented at least a token challenge to the rats. The room was permanently gloomy, as the two windows were covered with sandbags. They would be about as useful as a feather pillow if they took a direct hit but at least prevented shrapnel from exploding shells from screaming into the room.

It was pretty obvious that life at this OP was not exactly going to be a bed of roses and that a man could quickly go off his rocker if he did not learn to make use of the time the long periods of waiting incurred. I used this time to read books I had hitherto not had the time to plough through. I had some very interesting discussions with colleagues from countries near and far. For me, this was a golden opportunity to get on a more than nodding acquaintance with foreign customs and cultures. So in that respect, this self-inflicted internment was something of a privilege. Here I was, absorbing new information and new knowledge like a potato soaks up gravy and getting paid for it. But there were also periods of mind-numbing boredom when David and I took turns in sitting alone observing the bridge. And observing and observing. In fact, as there was no light, this was the only nocturnal activity available until it was your turn to sleep again. All cars drove with lights extinguished so as not to attract fire like candles attract moths. The whole area was blacked-out as well, so even for the most enthusiastic of observers there was little to see. It was a bit like trying to follow a black cat in a coal cellar at midnight. All you could do was to sit and stare into large expanses of nothing. The only thing that broke the sensory deprivation was the monotonous drone of cars crossing the bridge, which is probably why I remember this sound with such astonishing clarity. Dum-dum dum-dum as the rows of iron plates that formed the road surface hammered against each other in strict ballroom tempo as cars slowly crept across the 250m long bridge.

On my second watch on that first night at the OP, I had to fight to stay awake. I was struggling so much that I hoped the Serbs would start some form of kerfuffle so I would have something to do. If I am possessed of telepathic powers, I was soon to regret having used them. Suddenly, I head the characteristic shriek of an inbound artillery shell that exploded the very next second with a deafening, sharp, piercing crack which made it easy to visualise the shell's metal warhead disintegrating into thousands of lethal splinters. Seconds later, another was on its noisy way, landing 200m between the OP and the bridge. Both gave a brief but intense flash of light at the moment of detonation. It was the only light in seemingly endless darkness. Never before had I been spectator to artillery fire at such close range. In Mostar, mortar shells were the most common form of projectile, for which I now thanked my lucky stars. Artillery shells, I now knew, were much more powerful and destructive. Neither of the shells was fired with the primary purpose of destroying the bridge but to let the Croats know in no uncertain terms that the Serbs could achieve that task with pitiful simplicity at any time they chose. This sabre-rattling was an almost daily occurrence on both sides of the front line in Croatia. When I had gathered my wits and sat down again to continue my vigil in the dark night, I sent the Serbs a friendly thought and prayed they would rattle a bit closer to the Croatian positions the next time they felt the urge to flex their muscles.

A few hours later, I could delight in the spectacular sunrise from the restaurant's terrace. It was a breathtakingly beautiful sight to see the sun come dancing over the clifftops and be echoed in the glassy surface of a deep blue sea. It was a refreshing and uplifting contrast to the black of the night, which in the last long hours had palled beyond human endurance. Yet again, I was reminded of the contrasts life as a UNMO presented. Here, in the thick of things, the good and evil forces in life were stronger and more definable than

93

you can possibly experience from the comfort of your favourite armchair in front of the telly. I took a leisurely stroll along the low stone wall that led from the house to the western approach of the Maslenica Bridge 50 metres away. On the other side of this wall, there was a sheer drop of 40 metres. It would have been a beautiful sight had it not been for the piles of domestic rubbish that were piled on every outcrop of rock along the path. Some of the bridge piers were still standing, interlinked by twisted, tortured sculptures of iron that were once the road surface of the bridge. The crushed wreck of a car served as a memorial of the day the bridge was blown up. The car had been crossing the bridge as it happened, containing two unsuspecting victims that were hurled the nearly 50 metres down from the bridge, breaking almost every bone in their bodies but, astonishingly enough, living to tell the tale.

I peered down at the pontoon bridge, whose characteristic sound effects informed the world that traffic was crossing smoothly. As far as we could tell, about one vehicle in a hundred was military, the rest civilian. I speculated on what share of the traffic should be military before the bridge could be regarded as a military construction, as the Serbs claimed it was. Would 99% clinch the argument, or should it be 100%? And what was the status of the civilian trucks that transported food and supplies to the soldiers in the south? I was lost in my own thoughts when I heard a series of loud reports from the direction of the bridge. 'Here we go again,' I thought and started running towards the house. But this time, it was a false alarm. The explosions were caused by Croatian soldiers tossing sticks of dynamite into the river, presumably with the intention of deterring Serbian frogmen from planting explosive charges on the soft underbelly of the pontoon bridge. By the time I returned to the house to wake David, it was 0700 on the morning of 10 September, 1993. It was my turn to get some sleep.

The rest of the day was relatively peaceful in our immediate locality. In the late evening, the Serbs let us know they were still there by sending two artillery shells not too far away from us, which immediately triggered the adrenal glands into pumping their fight-or-flight fuel into the system. No damage was done to person or property, so it was another fit of sabre-rattling. Throughout the night, there was a constant low rumble from afar, with the horizon speckled with brief flashes of light. A massive exchange of fire across the front line was taking place somewhere. We made a report to the duty officer, who informed us that Zadar was under attack again. This was the second day running, which despite everything, was quite unusual. The *son-et-lumière* show we had been watching made us feel something significant had happened so we tried calling the office again. Our field telephone line was dead, probably because a shell had broken it somewhere. We were tempted to use the radio but it was policy that it should only be used for brief messages and we had no alternative but to wait until we were relieved the next day before we could get a background briefing.

In the two days David and I stood watch near the Maslenica Bridge, the situation throughout Sector South grew more and more critical. I learned that what had sparked off the attack on Zadar on 9 September was a full-blown infantry attack by units of the HV early that morning. They had re-taken territory near the village of Medak, not far from Gospić, some 60 km north of Zadar. This was the first time since January of that same year that anything on this scale had happened and the Serbian reaction came swiftly in the form of heavy and extensive bombardment of Croatian towns, of which Zadar was just one.

Over the next few days, the situation escalated almost hourly. Attack provoked counter-attack which provoked reprisal attack. It was a steep and slippery spiral. On 11 September, I followed developments on the radio. Reports from the team in Gospić made it clear that the situation in Sector North, our neighbouring sector, was also at boiling point, with large towns such as Sisak and Karlovac being bombarded. Not since the Croatian attack of January 1993 had hostilities been so violent. On that day, in Sector South alone, more than 6,000 shells were fired.

Throughout the day, the earth trembled as with a minor earthquake. The provincial town of Knin, proclaimed as the 'capital' of RSK[1] (Krajina) was attacked. This had never been done before because of the fear of reprisals against Zagreb. Which of the two towns was attacked first I am not sure, but the fact remains that on 11 September, 1993, the impossible happened. Until that time, Zagreb had slumbered like Sleeping Beauty but awoke that morning to a taste of the reality of war when a Frog-7 missile exploded in a suburb a few kilometres from the centre of town.

The last dramatic event that day before I left the office for my billet was that Jamal and the Norwegian Sten came bursting in. Half an hour earlier, they had left the Maslenica Bridge OP with undignified haste when the whole area started shaking to a sudden and heavy Serbian attack on both the bridge and its associated Croatian positions. This was the third occasion, but by no means the last, when Jamal had been so unlucky as to see Maslenica at its hottest. In the end, we teased him unmercifully for his misfortune and from then on when he left for the OP, it was with unkind choruses from the assembled company that we would make sure the Serbs were advised that the 'artillery magnet was on his way'.

There was a lot to enter in my diary that day and I closed with the following lines: 'I seem, yet again, to be in the thick of it. In the six weeks I have been in Sector South, it has changed from being the place where a major peace initiative in Croatia was to be launched to a theatre of total war. Being immersed in this witches' cauldron is a weird combination of utter terror and sheer excitement.'

Behind the scenes, a display of international power at the highest levels was unfolding. Who did what and who pressured whom I have no idea but international strings were most certainly pulled energetically in those days. On 12 September, Thorvald Stoltenberg[2] met President Tudjman, after which Generals Cot and Bobetko[3] put their heads together. UNPROFOR presented the two parties with a plan that involved a ceasefire and a Croatian withdrawal to the line as it was prior to the 9 September attacks.

This day was noticeably quieter than the previous day. At the Maslenica Bridge OP, bathed in glorious autumn sun, I summed up the events of the last few days:

> 'This is a strange war to be in. One day they fight like maniacs and shower each others soldiers and civilians with thousands of shells. The next day it is peaceful, the guns are silent and they get round the negotiation table. It will be interesting to see whether anything useful comes of it this time. But one thing is certain – the more bitter the fighting becomes, the more it will spread. And the more casualties there are to be on both sides, the more difficult it will be to negotiate a peaceful solution to the conflict. The growing mutual hatred as the war claims more and more victims is almost palpable.'

On 13 September, both sides accepted the UNPROFOR plan, whose conditions were to be implemented as soon as possible. Things did not get off to the best start. That same afternoon, hostilities flared up again. The pontoon bridge came under an attack that grew in ferocity until, at about 1900, the two UNMOs were forced to withdraw to safety. Shortly before, one of our Croatian liaison officers asked us to pass a message to the Serbs via our sector HQ in

*Mostar, June 1993: Shell-shattered buildings on the central stretch of the front line. On the left a building smoulders after a recent salvo. The road is littered with chunks of masonry, fallen telegraph poles, unexploded shells and ruined belongings.*

*Mostar, May 1993: A destroyed building at the central part of the front line.*

ABOVE
*Mostar, June 1993: 'Stari most' – the old bridge over the Neretva, damaged but still standing. It lay in the middle of the front line and was shelled to destruction in November 1993 after standing there for 427 years. Mount Hum is in the background.*

BELOW
*Mostar, May 1993: Spanish APC crossing the Tito bridge from East to West Mostar. It was still possible at that time to escort civilians across the front line. The flag of Bosnia-Herzegovina hangs over the street.*

*Mostar, May 1993: 'A Join the Army' poster from the 2nd HVO Brigade.*

*Mostar, June 1993: The dead body of a seven-year-old girl shot dead by a sniper. Together with three dead young men, she was in the hospital's mortuary waiting to be buried. The episode is described in the book.*

*Mostar, June 1993: Our host family in front of the house. From left: author and Irma, Meho's mother, Grant 'Kiwi' Finlayson, Nedija, Meho, Meho's eldest brother and their father, Tehir. Sitting in front: José Novak from Argentina and a nabo girl.*

*Mostar, June 1993: Mirza (Young) Humo – our Muslim liaison officer – and the author in a park that doubled as a cemetery, in East Mostar. To his left lies NN, a man found in the Neretva, minus his head. Young Humo was killed three weeks after this picture was taken.*

*Mostar, 18 June 1993: The author next to his car, safely in front of the house after receiving 12 direct hits. Under his left thumb is the entry hole of the bullet that missed his head by 20 cm.*

*Sector South, September 1993: The observation post – the Serbian latrine – at the Maslenica Bridge. The author standing at the door to his bed/dining/sitting room cum shelter, which has been cosily decorated with sandbags (right).*

*Medak Pocket, September 1993: Soldiers from the Canadian UN battalion in the village of Raicevici the morning after it, and all the other villages in the pocket, were destroyed by Croatian forces. Lt-Col Calvin stands in the middle.*

ABOVE
*Bihac Pocket, November 1993: Skokovi crossing after heavy snowfall.*

BELOW
*Krajina, December 1993: The Croatian village of Dreznikgrad in Serbian-controlled Krajina, razed to the ground and abandoned. Scenes like this were a common sight on the route through Krajina from Velika Kladusa to Bihac.*

ABOVE
*Bihac Pocket, December 1993: One of the daily meetings with Asim Delic at his spartan office in the Agrokomerc building. Delic is seated left. Next to him stands his chief of staff, a lawyer. The flag of Bosnia-Herzegovina hangs on the wall. The author is standing in the middle next to Sammi Odei and the Frenchman Lionel Gruhn.*

BELOW
*Bihac Pocket, January 1994: In the company of soldiers of 505 Brigade of Knights at the command post in Todorovo. The soldier, front row left, is displaying the Brigade's green collar. Next to him is the interpreter Aida, Nanic (the Brigade Commander's younger brother) and Harris Salem from Pakistan. The author is standing in the middle.*

ABOVE
*Bihac Pocket, January 1994: Norwegian Harald Bauck (right) and French platoon commander Gireaud observing Serbian positions on the hillsides near Bosanska Otoka, where the citizens spent their lives in the middle of a war zone.*

BELOW
*Bihac Pocket, January, 1994: Harald Bauck (left) in conversation with Gireaud. They are taking cover behind the house to the right. A French armoured récce vehicle is in the background.*

Knin: 'If the attack on Croat positions and civilian installation does not cease forthwith, this will be a day long remembered in Knin.' The message originated from the HV commander in Sector South territory. It was one of those threats that was easily made but difficult to fulfil and the attack continued unabated.

At about 2100, the north wing of the Hotel Kolovara was hit by a 120-mm mortar shell. (Our office was in the south wing.) Dominique from Switzerland and Peter from England were dispatched to determine what had happened. The sight that greeted them was not for the squeamish and they were both visibly shaken afterwards at their discovery. The shell had penetrated the wall without exploding and hit a woman in the head, obliterating it and leaving it as grisly morsels splattered over the wall nearby. A two-year-old boy lost the sight of one eye but survived. Peter and Dominique had to administer first aid to a number of deeply shocked victims who had been innocent bystanders to this horrendous incident.

Later that evening, the office informed us that I, and three other members of the team, had been ordered to be at two hours' readiness to reinforce our colleagues in Gospić in their efforts to implement the ceasefire agreement, in all likelihood coming into effect the next day. So I packed my gear and had a beer with Yunis – or rather I had a beer and he had a soft drink. Yunis was a Kenyan Somalian and therefore Muslim. He was one of the three others designated for the reinforcement task.

Sleep was frustratingly elusive that night. Thoughts of the new challenge the dawn would bring buzzed around inside my head, denying me sleep and rest. The last few days had convinced me that a successful outcome of this task was considered of paramount importance in the upper echelons of both the military and diplomatic UN leaders in former Yugoslavia. A breakthrough had to be made here and now – and I was to be part of it. But this Arthurian dream was not the only thing that kept me awake. The centre of Zadar was under heavy fire from artillery. Shell after shell came shrieking over the house I was living in and exploded with ear-splitting blasts a few hundred metres away. As long as they kept that up – flying over the house, that is – no, such speculation was pointless. If you once started thinking like that, you might as well 'pack up your troubles in your old kit bag' because your days as a UN Military Observer were numbered. The succession of freight trains roaring past over the house continued for what seemed like forever. It was not the most comfortable of sensations to know that the next one – or the one after that – could fall just slightly shorter than the ones before. As long as they kept going past. As long as the banshee wailing did not stop. Because as all soldiers know, it is the one that makes no noise that gets you. I had just come to love the shriek of the shells.

1. RSK – short for *Republika Srbska Krajina,* the Serbian Republic of Krajina, the self-proclaimed country of the Krajinan Serbs.
2. The UN's special envoy to former Yugoslavia.
3. Commanders-in-chief of UNPROFOR and HV.

## Chapter 8

# The Medak Pocket –
# Croatia Loses its Innocence

Through the rest of the night I was woken from time to time by a brace of shells flying overhead, but otherwise got a good night's sleep. But the next morning, as I was walking the 400 metres to the office, I was not feeling quite so chirpy. Freezing cold and accusing glances accompanied me all the way and at the hotel some of the refugees gave audible vent to their feelings. The UN received as thorough a verbal battering that morning as the Croatians had by bombardment the previous day. Unreasonable or not, that was the lot of someone at the coal face of that gigantic organisation.

In the afternoon it was finally confirmed that I and the three others were to set off for Gospić. The Croatian retreat was to take place as planned. Departure time was set at 1400 but the weather was causing problems. For fear of being accused of not being impartial, the UN did not use the Maslenica floating bridge but a bridge, that was by now getting worn out, to the island of Pag. From here, there was a ferry to the mainland, some 20 minutes away. Over the last few days, the wind had been blowing hard from the north and the flat-bottomed ferries had difficulty manoeuvring in the choppy water. If the ferries were taken out of operation, there was only one road to the north and that was over the floating bridge which the Croatians had frequently asked the UN to make use of and thereby extend some form of passive protection. Up to now, their requests had been categorically refused. The UN had no intention of allowing themselves to be used as a shield or a hostage. But today an exception was made. The operation in the north was of overriding importance, so if the ferries could not sail, principles had to be temporarily abandoned. We would have to take the punishment for our intransigence

– either in the form of shells or later as indignant protests from the Serbs. But we had to get north, come what may.

We were in regular contact with the Croatian authorities, most recently at 1400, when it became clear the ferries were still operating. So we drove to Gospić via Pag with no problems but had to contend with a very bumpy crossing. Gospić was a medium sized town just behind the front line and had been badly damaged by the heavy mortar and artillery attacks it been subjected to.

Shortly before, it had been evacuated for fear of chemical warfare in the area. This was a threat that caused concern throughout the UN contingent and I made sure my gas mask was firmly attached to my flak jacket. The Danish UN observers, incidentally, were among the few to be supplied with gas-masks. Yunis had never even held one in his hands. Many of the other observers requested help from UNPROFOR to get hold of a supply but were informed it was a matter for the national forces to deal with. Meanwhile, they had to live with the threat that was never far from the surface and hope for the best. The gas-mask story was by no means an isolated incident and is an excellent illustration of the difference there was between the various national contingents in how well-equipped their troops were for this UN mission, which, in many ways, distanced itself from those before it. In this respect, the Danish soldiers were among the most well prepared, both in terms of equipment and training.

The team's office, just under two kilometres from the centre of town, had so far been spared a direct hit, but there had been near-misses aplenty, the last just two days previously when the building opposite had taken a battering. Our office, indeed the whole building, was very primitive and reminded me of conditions on the Serbian side of the front line. But on a professional level, from the very start we were on the same wavelength as the Gospić team, with whom we would be working closely throughout the operation. Our SMO, the Danish Lieutenant-Colonel Ove Nielsen, arrived in Gospić to run the UNMO side of things personally. Fréderic, the French team leader, gave us a detailed briefing of the area and the current situation.

The Croatian Army consisted largely of relatively well-equipped units, manned mostly by recruits from the local areas they were defending. There was a wide age difference in the units and their uniforms appeared to be rather the opposite, more customised is perhaps the best word. In addition, HV had a number of 'professional' brigades, consisting almost exclusively of well-trained and well-disciplined young men. These units were superbly equipped and seldom played a stationary role. They were usually kept in reserve for insertion in strategic operations or to stabilise a volatile section of a difficult front. They were all called by the names of animals – Tiger, Cobra and Wolf, for example – and membership of their ranks was proudly displayed to the world by embroidered badges the size of a clenched fist.

It was the Wolves who had attacked and taken the 8 × 10 km of territory south of Gospić on 9 September, an area that up to that date had been a Serbian pocket surrounded on the north, west and south by HV units. Whether the timing of the offensive – the ninth day of the ninth month – had anything to do with the fact that the Wolves were the HV's 9th Brigade, I am not certain, but it is an interesting coincidence.

The area was known to the UN as the Medak Pocket, named after a village close by. What the strategic thinking behind the attack was remained undisclosed, but there were many theories. The most grandiose was that it was the first phase of a major offensive on the Gospić-Gračac-Knin axis intended to split southern Krajina in two. At any rate, the lid was put on the plan with the Croatian assent to transfer control of the area to UNPROFOR.

The actual transfer of control was the responsibility of a Canadian UN battalion, reinforced by two French companies. It was rumoured that the French were included after a direct order from UNPROFOR's Commander-in-Chief, General Cot, himself a Frenchman. The tricolour would also be flying at the front during Operation Medak, as it had been dubbed.

Whatever the circumstances, it would not be out of place here to comment that UNPROFOR's flexibility and effectiveness seemed to me to be reduced from time to time because of the superpower national pride of certain European countries. It seemed to me that the British and French contingents worked more closely with their national governments than they did with their UN commanders in the field. That is in no way meant to belittle their contribution or their professionalism, more a comment on the attitude they occasionally displayed towards this special task. The contingents from the smaller countries seemed to be more sympathetic to the fact that, temporarily at least, they were under UN command first and national command second.

The plan for UNPROFOR's takeover of the area was straight-forward enough and consisted of four phases (see map section):

Phase 1: A Canadian and a French company would replace the Serbs in their front-line positions facing the Medak Pocket. In parallel with this – and before Phase 3 – the Military Observers, with the assistance of Croatian liaison officers, were to determine the exact front line as it was prior to the attack on 9 September.

Phase 2: The Canadians, who normally operated in the area under Serbian control, would then establish a corridor through the Croatian lines, so that, together with the other French company, they could start deployment in the pocket itself.

Phase 3: The Croats should be replaced in their current front-line positions by one Canadian company with the French company occupying the front line by 9 September.

Phase 4: The full withdrawal of Croatian forces from the pocket, monitored by the Canadian battalion. At the same time a sweep team was to go through the area with a fine-tooth comb for any wounded and Serbs still in the pocket.

The plan was the initiative of UNPROFOR and sanctioned by both parties. It was to go into operation on the afternoon of 15 September and be completed 24 hours later. On that same afternoon, a Polish UNMO and I drove to a temporary helicopter pad to pick up the Canadian Colonel Maissoneuve who had flown from the Zagreb HQ. He was in command of all UNPROFOR's operations and had come to be in a situation to take quick decisions in the field should it be necessary. His very presence was yet another signal of how important UNPROFOR HQ regarded the operation. Later that day, General Stepitic of the general staff in Zagreb also arrived. Everything was ready. Operation Medak could begin.

The operation started according to plan but quickly ran into problems. As soon as the Serbs had been replaced at their front-line positions by the Canadians, the Croats began shooting at the UN soldiers with small arms and heavy machine-guns, in some cases even cannon. We got the impression they were shooting to scare the troops and hamper the operation rather than with intent to kill. Whatever the reason, the Canadians returned the fire bullet by bullet and laid down the line for the rest of the operation. They suffered no casualties during this exchange of fire. Shortly after midnight, Phase 2 was complete and an opening in the Croatian front line had been created at the village of Licki Ribnik, some seven kilometres south-east of Gospić. From this village, the road ran due south into the Medak Pocket. It was along this road, the only paved road in the area, that the two companies would proceed at noon the following day.

The next morning, 16 September, I and all the other UNMOs drove over to the Croatian HQ in Gospić to pick up our liaison officers. We would then together determine the boundaries of the pocket, which corresponded roughly to the line of 9 September, and set the limits of the Canadian advance accordingly. My primary function was to act as adjutant to Maissoneuve, who was in constant contact with SMO, the commander of the Canadian battalion and General Cot at UNPROFOR HQ. It was a busy job, with situations constantly arising that demanded our attention. For example, we received an urgent message from the Canadians who had taken the Serbian positions, claiming that explosions had been heard deep inside the pocket. Brigadier Ademi, commanding the HV forces in the area and directly responsible for their withdrawal, was contacted but he earnestly reassured us that the explosions were simply the result of minefield clearance.

At about the same time, a serious problem arose. The Croats took us all by surprise and demanded that the original plan be adjusted so that the UN troops should not occupy the line of 9 September and the current front line simultaneously. Their demand was for them to take the current front line and then progress, step by step, from east to west at the same pace as the Croatian withdrawal. Attempts to persuade them to stick to the original plan failed and UNPROFOR had to concede and the plan was adjusted accordingly. At the same time, we were informed that the Croatian withdrawal had been postponed by 24 hours. Who made this decision and why, I have no idea. My guess is that UNPROFOR wanted to avoid fighting fire with fire for fear that the Croats would dig their heels in and refuse to move at all, thus stalling the operation. Everyone had great expectations that Operation Medak would mark the beginning of something on a much larger scale, in line with the Blue Zones I mentioned earlier that came to nothing.

To begin with, the Croats' motives were not clear but became more and more obvious as the day went on. 'Minefield clearance' in the pocket continued at a brisk pace, and although many mines had undoubtedly been laid, the number of explosions recorded was ridiculously out of proportion to the number of mines it would have been necessary to detonate to facilitate a withdrawal. The only conclusion open to us was that they were blowing up other things as well.

At 1200, when the Canadians were scheduled to drive through the breach in the Croatian front line and deploy along the actual front line, the next problem arose. The Croats would not let them pass. The Canadians insisted, to use polite language, and demanded the Croatians remove the impromptu roadblock they had made with two tanks. No response. The Canadians readied two rocket launchers so they could fight their way through if necessary. Yunis, who was right on the spot with Dominique at the time, later described the situation as 'like a bow pulled to breaking point that could snap at any moment with a terrifying crack'. If the Canadians and Croats had engaged each other there would most assuredly have been casualties. The tension lasted for several nerve-racking minutes as Yunis and Dominique poured oil on the troubled waters. They succeeded and the Canadian rocket launchers were traversed to a safe bearing, the Croatian tanks removed and, an hour delayed, the Canadian company rolled into the Medak Pocket.

Not long afterwards, more problems were encountered with the Croats slowing down the Canadians in their efforts to push further towards the of line 9 September. They were able to set the pace of the advance, despite valiant Canadian efforts to speed it up. At about the same time, HV protested the fact that no UN troops had yet been deployed in the mountainous south-east corner of the pocket as agreed, and until that situation had been rectified they would stop all withdrawal. This caused some considerable confusion as the Canadians firmly believed they had already taken that area and had occupied it for some time. Eventually they were able to confirm this and the Croats had no alternative but to accept it. But in the thirty minutes it had taken to unravel this Gordian knot, no progress had been made in the advance.

The Croats continued their operation 'Spanner-in the-Works' and out of the blue demanded a conference with the UN Head of Civilian Affairs for former Yugoslavia. Their pretext was 'to discuss terms of who might have access to the area after HV had evacuated it'. Until that conference took place, with a satisfactory outcome, all Croatian withdrawal activity would cease. Nothing even verging on this topic had been mentioned during the initial stages of the operation and it would have been more natural for it to be an extension of the military operation anyway. Nevertheless, a representative of the UN Head of Civilian Affairs was flown with great haste to Gospić. To pre-empt further delays, she was given strict orders, under no circumstances, to negotiate before the HV withdrawal but to hold herself ready at immediate notice. After some discussion, the Croats accepted these terms and the operation, even more delayed, could proceed. It was around this time that I began to suspect the Croats' delaying tactics were part of a predetermined plan with a specific objective.

By late afternoon, the Canadians had reached the two most easterly small villages in the pocket and saw with their own eyes the 'minefields' the Croats had told us about. The villages were razed to the ground with dynamite and anti-tank mines. When he saw what had happened and could hear what was still going on to the west, the Canadian battalion commander asked for permission to press on his deployment with force to preserve whatever was left standing. His request was denied, in my opinion because the HQ commander believed the price of such an action to be too high. Maissoneuve tried to put an end to the wanton destruction through the auspices of the Croatian general accompanying him but, to his great frustration, with no success. As darkness fell, the Canadians were in position at the current front line, the entire length of which was now occupied by UN troops. They had also reached a point three kilometres inside the pocket and had deployed in a north-south line, ready to continue their advance at sunrise.

In the UNMO building in Gospić, we were delighted with the day's achievements, made under extremely difficult conditions, but regretful that the Croats' tour of pillage and devastation could not have been stopped. The extent of the damage would have been minimised if the Canadians' request had been approved but it would certainly have cost UN soldiers' lives. A terrible decision, for which I do not envy those responsible.

The same evening, the SMO ordered the Pole Kaziemierz and I to drive to the Canadian battalion to act as liaison officers between the two the following day. By midnight, Kaz and I had reached the village of Raicevici, where the command HQ had been set up. The damage lay under the cover of darkness and we could only guess at its extent. We bivouacked close to the command APC, having asked for an early shake so we could be up and ready to go at dawn.

I slept under a night sky that was as black as pitch and bursting with countless bright stars – under less extreme circumstances it would been very romantic. As I lay snuggled in my sleeping bag, I became more and more annoyed at the thick clouds of tobacco smoke billowing out of the back of the APC. Wisps of smoke sneaked up my nose as I lay half asleep and after an hour I could stand it no more. I crawled out of my sleeping bag to ask politely if they could ration their baccy and discovered to my astonishment that nobody in the APC was smoking. Then I realised that the thick swathes of smoke were being wafted over my primitive camp from the burned-out houses hidden in the darkness.

At one point in the depths of night, the field telephone rang. It was an interpreter informing the duty officer that Brigadier Ademi wanted an immediate conference with the Canadian battalion commander, Calvin. But Calvin was less than enthusiastic at the prospect of a night meeting with the man who had slowed him down so frustratingly throughout the previous day. Soon after, the duty officer woke Calvin again to tell him that if he would not agree to a meeting immediately, Ademi would call the operation off. At that time, I had not met Calvin but I was later to learn that his answer to the ultimatum was very characteristic of the man. 'Tell him to fuck off. Maybe I'll meet him tomorrow . . . maybe!' The duty officer cleared his throat and asked tentatively whether Calvin was sure it would be wise to reject the request so out of hand. 'Yes, I am. Now don't bother me with this question any more.' As I heard this exchange, I began to get a picture of the man I was to get to know as a real 'warrior' – and a hopeless diplomat.

The sight that greeted my eyes when I woke up shortly before dawn was not a pretty one. Raicevici lay just 100 metres from the small, grassy plateau where I had slept. It was battered to the ground. Every house in that little community, about thirty in all, had been blown up and burned. The ruins were still standing, smouldering and with the odd flame still bursting greedily into life as it found a lump of wood it had not yet consumed. There was no trace of life, nothing alive – not a dog, not a chicken. A clammy blanket of death enveloped what had once been a lively settlement ensconced in beautiful countryside, clumps of trees and green fields, with a view of the mountains to the south. But I was soon to discover more. In a burned-out collapsed barn, I found the charred corpses of several cows, tethered to the fallen remains of the walls of the barn by chains which stretched their necks out, as if bellowing at those that had burned them alive. But this sad sight paled into insignificance compared to what the Canadians found later that day in the ruins of this village and other places in the Medak Pocket.

At sunrise, the advance continued and the pattern of the previous day was repeated. The Canadians pushed and the Croats pushed back. The result was a slow but sure move forward. Calvin, who was an officer bursting with energy, was constantly on the move and his sheer determination and will-power worked like a locomotive pushing everything around him relentlessly forward. The Croats could not do anything without him breathing down their necks and full advantage was taken of their slightest falter. Sometimes, I felt he was struggling not to toss his blue helmet down the mountainside and get on with the job in a proper, warlike fashion, free of the bonds that distinguish a UN operation from a military mission. At 1200 I was sure of it.

Shortly before, the Serbs had asked us to go to the assistance of some Serbian soldiers and civilians who were still in the area and had sought shelter in the forest-clad mountains to the south. They had desperately radioed in that they were being pursued by Croatian patrols. Calvin held a brief meeting with Ademi in which they sorted out some disagreements that had arisen over details of how the operation should proceed. I observed this discussion from a distance of 25 metres but I had no problem following their discussion, which was not exactly conducted *sotto voce*. Threats and harsh words flowed from both mouths. Information on the fleeing Serbs and stories of macabre discoveries of murdered people were beginning to come out. Calvin responded in true character and said to Ademi, nose to nose, 'If we find those bastards who blow up houses and kill people, we will shoot them. They are a disgrace to the Croatian Army!' Calvin was far too professional ever to do anything of the sort but that was the sort of speech his tongue was created for. He was an outstanding officer, perhaps even brilliant, but as a diplomat he was a disaster. A UN officer is required to have at least some command of that difficult skill, so he still had something to learn.

In the course of the day, the tempo speeded up and the teamwork between the UNMOs and the Canadians began to work like clock-work. Before any move forward, the UNMOs drove ahead, made a quick recce and smoothed the way for the Canadian advance. If they had problems, they let me or Kaz know and we immediately informed Calvin so he could constantly fine-tune his decisions. It was all working beautifully and towards the end of the day a few words of grateful recognition were tossed from the mouth of this talented, but very independent, officer.

As the Canadians pushed their way forward deeper into the pocket, it became all too apparent that every house along the way had suffered the same fate as those in Raicevici. Everything in sight was razed to the ground. During the day, we must have passed through every village and hamlet in the pocket and in most places there was abundant evidence that the Serbs had abandoned their homes in panic. In front of one house, a group of soldiers must have been eating their breakfast when the attack started. Everything was in place, just as they had left it when they dashed from their table. There was a chunk of bread half bitten through – which tells better than any words how quickly they must have moved. Everything pointed to the fact that the Serbs had been taken completely by surprise, a deduction that was later confirmed by survivors interrogated by UN personnel. In and around the ravaged houses, lay haphazard piles of belongings that the Serbs had had to leave behind and which the Croats had not had the time to plunder because of the tempo with which Operation Medak, despite all the attempts to delay it, had been conducted.

The entire region was a typical farming community – small villages linked by potholed gravel paths and dirt roads. On each side of these were the fields that also acted as boundaries to the villages, which despite their size were nonetheless small, autonomous communities. It struck me that the life which had gone on here before the tidal wave of destruction had remained virtually unchanged for centuries. It was unlikely that the birthplace of dreams of independence, war and ethnic annihilation would be found here, but it was here that the price had been paid.

Like all front-line areas in former Yugoslavia, there were extensive minefields. This was one of the reasons why we UNMOs, in our unarmoured vehicles, were restricted to paved roads, where it was more difficult to conceal mines. But plans were one thing and expediency another. In the Medak Pocket there were almost no paved roads and if we were to be of any use at all, we had to compromise our own safety. We had been given sketches from both the Serbs and the Croats indicating the roads were not mined but they were pretty rudimentary and we felt far from secure with them in our pockets. It was an especially dangerous situation when we met a UN vehicle coming towards us on the same road that was too narrow to allow two vehicles to pass. We could choose between reversing for kilometres and accepting the inherent delay, or driving off the road and keeping our fingers crossed. We took the chance but with our hearts in our mouths every time. I saw a French APC do the same and it detonated a mine just as it was passing another vehicle. That gamble cost two wounded soldiers. It was only by luck the price was not higher. If the vehicle driving over the mine had not been armoured, there would have been several fatalities.

The sweep team was working flat out, partly in the hunt for survivors and partly to gain a complete picture of the destruction. It was dirty and dangerous work and in their searches of the ruins the threat of booby-trapped mines was always present. These were seemingly innocent affairs of which troops had to be constantly aware. One day a soldier searching a house moved a mattress that was in his way. It was attached by wire to a mine.

The result of their searches was horrifying and when I heard about it, I could not overcome my disbelief. Twenty or so charred bodies were found in or near the burned houses. A few were soldiers but most of them were old people that had not been able to move fast enough. Their bodies were examined by doctors to determine the cause of death. The soldiers had probably been killed in action, but the civilian corpses had a different story to tell. Some were shot whilst running away, others at very close range in the head. Others had no bullet wounds and were killed inside the collapsing, burning buildings or simply burned alive. One or two were found that had not been burned. One of these was a man found on a narrow path leading away from his ruined house. He had eight bullet wounds in his head and 24 in his back. Another was a woman found near Raicevici, where I had spent the night. She had three bullet wounds in the right side of her body and a deep knife wound in her chest. Both her legs were broken. Another woman was found lying in a small grass field close to the ruins of a house. She had been shot in the back of the head at close range. Her face had entirely disappeared.

The damage to property, which seems irrelevant compared to descriptions such as these, was enormous. More than 300 houses and barns were completely destroyed. Dead livestock and oil had been thrown into countless wells. If the area was ever to be inhabited again, it would have to be totally rebuilt.

At 1500, a team of reporters from the Croatian H-TV asked for an interview with Calvin on Operation Medak. He was not prepared to waste his time on such things and they had to make do with his second-in-command. Half an hour later, when a team from Reuters made the same request, Calvin was more than forthcoming. In his answer, he did not mince words in his description of the destruction and what it concealed. Operation Medak became the lead story on Canadian TV news that evening.

Around 1800, the last Canadian and French troops were in

position on the front line of 9 September and the last of the Croatian troops out of the area. The Medak Pocket was now under full UN control, in full accordance with the modified plan. This marked the end of the UNMO part of the operation. We all overnighted in Gospić and next morning set off for our respective sectors. A challenging and extremely interesting operation was over.

For the Canadian soldiers, there was still some way to go. The final positions of Croatian and Canadian troops on each side of the line of 9 September line still had to be settled in negotiations between Calvin and Ademi, which, not unexpectedly did not take place without problems. A final search of the whole pocket was also to be undertaken to ensure all bodies had been discovered. During this task, a small group of Serbs emerged from the tree-covered mountains in the south. They were clearly relieved to bump into UN troops and not Croatian soldiers and after interrogation were handed over to the Krajina Serbian authorities.

At the end of September, a war crimes commission visited the Medak Pocket on a fact-finding mission to determine any legal consequence for the perpetrators of alleged atrocities. Independent of this event, General Ademi had been accused of being directly responsible for the massacre that had taken place in the pocket and a few weeks later was relieved of command. The question remaining was whether it really was Ademi who had single-handedly planned and executed the campaign of systematic destruction or whether the order had come from someone higher up in the military, or even political, system who now preferred to remain anonymous when faced with his atrocities.

While all this was going on, a number of Serbian survivors were being questioned by the UN. They confirmed that the Serbian soldiers had been totally unprepared for the attack and had been unable to put up sufficient resistance to give the civilians time to escape. Eyewitness accounts from civilian survivors were horrific, telling of the shooting of escaping civilians, summary executions and people being burned alive. There is always a risk that such accounts are fabrications but the Canadian discoveries had made it highly probable that the witnesses were, unfortunately, telling the truth.

Operation Medak also featured in the Croatian media, and considering the censorship it was rumoured they worked under, with an openness that was surprising. On 21 September, the newspaper *Slobodna Dalmacija* quoted General Cot for making the following statement after a visit to the Medak Pocket: 'I haven't seen any sign of life in several villages we visited today. The destruction is complete, systematic and intentional.' In my eyes that is a remarkably clear message and leads me to believe that either the censorship was not as strict as rumoured or the article was run by a brave editor.

The contribution of the UN forces to Operation Medak won the acclaim of various offices in the UN organisation. That it was accomplished at all was regarded as a remarkable achievement, bearing in mind the difficulties that were encountered along the way. Particular respect was won for the ability to make the Croats stick to the modified schedule. A few days after we had returned to Zadar, General Cot, the UNPROFOR commander, sent the following fax to everyone that had been involved in the operation:

> 'Mr Thorvald Stoltenberg, special representative of the Secretary General to former Yugoslavia, has asked me to express to you his satisfaction with the manner in which the Medak-Gospić operation was executed. I would also like to congratulate all of you for your professionalism and courage.'

Although Operation Medak was a success in itself, it did not mark the pivotal point in the conflict that had been hoped in the UN. Hostilities continued with shooting on both sides of the front-line positions and bombardment of civilian targets in the towns. To me a solution to the conflict seemed further away than ever when I heard how vehemently the Serbs let it be known that, in the wake of Operation Medak and in the event that they would ever consider laying down their arms, they would never trust any guarantees for fair play from the Croatian Government.

But the operation was a turning point for me, at least, in my understanding of the conflict in Croatia. I could now appreciate that Croatia was not merely an innocent victim of local Serbian aggression, as I had heard so many times from the Croats, but was not without blame itself. The country, which so dearly wished to regain those areas that had been amputated, had now shown that it was prepared to use every means to achieve it, even those that should have disappeared with Ghengis Khan. To me, then, Croatia lost its innocence with Operation Medak and was now on a standing with the other warring parties, including those with the worst reputations in Bosnia-Herzegovina. That this massacre, in its brutality a match for those known from Kriz and Stupni Do[1] in Bosnia, did not cost Croatia its international goodwill remains a mystery to me and must probably be put down to very skilful diplomacy. But when it comes to Croatia's international reputation and their desire to join the ranks of the countries of the west, I sincerely hope that those responsible for the outrage – high and low alike – will be made to answer for their actions.

1. Kriz, near Prozor in Bosnia-Herzegovina, September 1993. Thirty-five civilians were massacred, allegedly by Armija BiH soldiers. Stupni Do, also in Bosnia-Herzegovina, October 1993. A Muslim village in HVO-controlled territory was attacked and the civilian population massacred.

# Chapter 9

# Zadar – Hot and Hostile Ceasefire

We were not permitted to rest on our laurels for long. Only four days later, at 1300 on 21 September, our Croatian liaison officers began their protests against the Serbian bombardment of a number of villages close to the front line, including a few near Zemunik Airport. Once again, it is important to stress that the reason protests were made at all was because there was supposed to be a ceasefire in effect. We got in touch with our colleagues at Sector HQ in Knin to hear their assessment of the reasons underlying the Serbian attacks. Knin, as it turns out, was up to its ears in protests from the Serbs against Croatian shelling of Serb-controlled front-line towns east of Zadar. Everything indicated that it was another of the now normal and tedious violations of this ill-fated ceasefire. At 1320, from our office in the Hotel Kolovara, I heard the detonation of seven artillery shells in Zadar itself and began to think that the situation may be developing into something more serious. Time seemed to stand still. Protests were now arriving in a steady flow, with the intermittent staccato thud of shells falling around town, but there was no escalation of hostilities for the next two hours. In the meantime, together with HQ at Knin, we tried to persuade the Croats and Serbs to check fire, without much success. It was like being at the pit of a cockfight, where the cocks were doing little other than strutting about, sizing each other up but could, at any second, start pecking each others eyes out.

At 1515 exactly, the fuse burned out and the explosion occurred. A hailstorm of artillery shells showered down on the centre of Zadar and its suburbs. In the next 15 minutes, I counted 50 explosions, about half of which sounded as though they came from the centre, about 500m from the office. It was all a bit tense for a while, as we sat in our flak jackets and battle helmets waiting to see what fate had in store for us that day. We considered moving to the cellar in case

113

the hotel received another direct hit but decided to stick it out and maintain contact with Knin, from where our ever-energetic SMO was fighting a valiant fight to bring a halt to the outbreak of hostilities.

In the midst of all this action, we received a fax from Knin ordering us to man the OP at Zemunik Airport from 1800 to follow developments in the ceasefire the SMO was trying to arrange. It was an order that raised our eyebrows in astonishment. It came from an otherwise professional and sensible operations officer who, however, had never been to the airport, as was obvious from his order. Zemunik lay right on the front line and was frequently under heavy attack, as it had already been that day. The OP was situated at the top of the control tower, where the view was as excellent as the protection it afforded was appalling. Outside, the tower was pock-marked with shrapnel scars – inside, it was a wreck. The only shelter the building offered was the cellar, which, not unusually, was some distance from the control room itself. Access to the cellar was down a steep, rickety and, in places, missing spiral staircase with no bannister. At night, tackling these stairs without a torch was suicidal and it was by night, that very night, that we were to make the attempt. Going down those stairs at night and in a hurry would be just as dangerous as staying in the control room and observing. If things got uncomfortably hot in this kamikaze post, there was only one thing to do – cross your fingers and hope for the best. We were on the verge of giving Knin a sharp lesson in the realities of life at this far-flung outpost of its territory when our liaison officer made it unnecessary. They would not allow us to use the OP.

Not long after the nail-biting tension of the ferocious attack on the centre of Zadar, things quietened down somewhat. Front-line positions were still under fire but the town itself was only occasionally a direct target. And so it continued until about 1800, when fire at the other end of the front line ceased altogether.

That evening, I had dinner in the hotel's restaurant in the cellar. It was divided into a restaurant proper and a cafeteria. The restaurant was closest to the entrance and was for paying guests only. As these had been few and far between since the beginning of the war, it had been reduced to a handful of tables laid for four. In the much larger cafeteria, semi-partitioned off from the restaurant, the tables were arranged in long lines, ready to provide the hotel's many refugees with three square meals a day at set times. Watching this flood of people burst through the door as soon as it was flung open,

114

hand in their meal ticket, fill their bellies and retreat to their small rooms all in the space of 15 minutes was a depressing sight. Many of them had been living this meaningless, regimented life for almost two years and their listless behaviour betrayed the absence of any spark of life. This silent procession of *les misérables* past the tables was the best reason I can give for seldom using the restaurant.

Over the next couple of weeks or so, hostilities continued with varying intensity, concentrated mostly on front-line positions but occasionally swelling to take in the larger towns on both sides of the front line. Each such escalation unleashed a torrent of protests from both sides. They were delivered by hand, printed on dedicated forms with the heading 'PROTEST' in bold and were passed on to the opposing party via the UNMO office on that side of the front line. The protest form had spaces for a description of where the violation had taken place, where it was estimated the fire had originated and whether UNMOs could provide confirmation of the claims. This, of course, was our prime function and we were supposed to do this with every single violation of the ceasefire agreement in effect. In practice, however, in a phase of such massive bombardment, it would have required a small army of UNMOs to do the job to the letter of the law and not the spirit. Gradually, neither side regarded front-line attacks as anything out of the ordinary and the visit of a liaison officer was often prefaced with 'I have a protest for you – but it's only a front line violation'.

Despite this acceptance of realism, there were piles of protests which assumed a comical aspect, irrespective of the seriousness of the situation. I have lost count of the number of occasions on which a protest concluded with the empty threat, 'Take this as a last warning'. In the end, we UNMOs began referring to 'so-called cease-fire violations' that were so frequent as to imply war in southern Croatia had broken out again. Officially, that is, and a war that was stationary with no movement of the front line. If I had to describe the situation, it would be as a hot and hostile ceasefire pursued with rigid flexibility – a contradiction in terms that seems very fitting.

There were, though, violations that were taken very seriously every time – attacks on civilian targets, mostly in larger towns. Protests against such actions were followed up every time and an explanation demanded of the guilty party. Often we were told that the shelling had been carried out by the protesters themselves in an effort to gain public sympathy, a non-accidental own-goal. Technically, there was nothing to prevent either side from training their guns and opening fire from an angle that would make it seem as if it was the enemy that was responsible. Understandably, we were very sceptical about accusations of such morally reprehensible behaviour, but if there were a grain of truth in just one of them, then the conflict had taken a decidedly bizarre turn.

We UNMOs worked seven days a week for four weeks, after which we were given six days off. This work routine meant that our Croatian liaison officers, who had to accompany us on all our patrols, never had a day off. They solved the problem creatively and elegantly. They nominated Saturday as 'administration day', reserved for office work only. The knock-on effect of their neat thinking was that we were prevented from conducting any front-line patrols on Saturdays. Considering we were in the middle of a war zone, this was a rum situation but we had grown accustomed to so many strange goings-on that were never mentioned at staff college that we shrugged our shoulders and made use of the Saturdays to take a look at areas we otherwise would not have wasted our time on.

In early October, a Brazilian colleague and I were on a 'Saturday patrol' on the coast, heading for Split to confirm rumours of large Croatian troop movements. We saw nothing. But we did have a fabulous drive along the Adriatic, enjoying the warm sun on a day where there was not a breath of wind. We stopped at a bathing jetty, took off our boots and splashed around like ten-year-olds. Had it not been for the uniforms and the white UN car, it was a picture that could have come straight from a holiday catalogue. As I wrote up my diary that evening at about 2200, I had just managed to enter, 'The day has been perfectly idyllic . . .', when a shell flying overhead brought me cruelly back to the real world. The shell exploded somewhere in the middle of town. 'And goodnight to you,' I was thinking as another shell screamed overhead. BOOOM! Another explosion from a different part of town, and another and another and another. Another shell roared past, exploding only a few hundred metres away. 'This sounds serious,' I muttered to myself as I clambered into my flak jacket and helmet. The street outside was thronging with frightened people and though I had been taken by surprise just as much as they had been, the blue helmet was regarded as an automatic source of information.

'Why?' asked my neighbour, whose Bavarian accent gave away the fact he had spent some time working in Munich.

'I don't know,' I replied, in an attempt to stop the dialogue right there.

'What's going on today?' He was a persistent little neighbour.

'Nothing much,' I answered, knowing full well he would try and pump me for all I did not have.

A new shell that landed somewhere near the hotel gave me the excuse to nip inside again. It continued like this for the next hour, one shell screaming and exploding close by, the next some distance away. The earth was shaking and the air vibrating as if we were in the middle of some infernal thunderstorm. Forty-five times I counted the air being sucked by the vacuum created by a shell, sitting indoors in full battle kit, impotent to do anything but keep my fingers crossed. Just as unexpectedly as it had all started, it stopped. What sparked off this rude lullaby is a mystery but by morning the casualty list it had produced was finalised – one dead dog. Another miracle witnessed. Each one of the shells that had thundered past in the nightmare of that night could have killed many people.

The final entry in my diary was made at midnight and states that the day had brought a touch of beauty into a troubled spot, only to be ousted by a foaming fit of madness. This crazy combination reflects very well the contrasts of my life in Zadar.

At the foot of the OP at the Maslenica Bridge there was a river valley, shaped like a fat-bellied fish struggling to make the Adriatic. At the bulge of the belly, some 4 km south of the OP was the town of Novigrad, which in pre-war days had been the home of the rich, the Beverley Hills of the Balkans, with luxurious villas ensconced among beautiful mountains and a marina on the verge of over-crowding on a river that flowed into the Adriatic not so far away. But Novigrad's days of wine and roses were past and the town now marked the most forward of the Croatian front lines, with all the ensuing, almost daily, punishment this unenviable location brought with it. I made a single patrol of this outpost. The villas were battered, empty shells, the yachts lay with their keels in the air, the telephone poles were splintered like matchsticks and the streets were ankle deep in rubble and exclusive, but now shattered, personal belongings. Novigrad was like a stately home in an advanced state of decay, whose proud days of grandeur were unmistakable. An air of tension gripped the whole town because of the frequent artillery attacks, so the soldiers moved around with quick, scurrying steps from one source of cover to another to avoid being caught in the open if a raid started. Swedish Per-Gunnar and I sympathised with their feelings, did what we had come to do and left as quickly as possible with all the dignity we could muster. It was a wise move. A few minutes later, the town was reeling once more under a new barrage, with a rhythm from our safe distance that had the same monotonous and momentous tattoo as the drums that escort a condemned man to the scaffold.

From Novigrad we drove east to Suhovara, another village that had to take the blows when the Serb artillery handed out its systematic beating of front-line civilisation. Suhovara had none of Novigrad's wealth and elegance. It was a typical farming village, with small, spartan houses straddling dusty, unpaved roads. Scarred and battered as Suhovara was from its punishment for being situated just behind the front line, it was still inhabited, mostly by older people, who were always the last to abandon their homes.

In the middle of the village, we passed an old man leading a flock of sheep to their pasture. That day, he could easily have been the next victim of the shells that every now and then fell on his village. He knew it better than most but seemed to have accepted the situation with astonishing calm as he strolled down the road with a straw hanging from the corner of his mouth. In this grim situation, this touch of normality had an element of the bizarre but I had grown used to it and had long ago ceased to be surprised at what people could get accustomed to and just accept as part of everyday life.

A little further down the road, we came across a ramshackle old cottage, one end of which had taken a hit from a mortar shell. At the door, stood an old woman surveying a world she had given up trying to understand. Not even our arrival could ignite any spark of life in her absent gaze, a visible symptom of the fact that her mind was unable or unwilling to come to terms with the conflict that had disrupted a natural and lifelong rhythm.

In the nearby HQ of the Croat unit responsible for the defence of the area, we were welcomed cordially enough but they could not give us any information we did not already have. Their sitrep – that their troops were holding a front line that never moved and that they frequently came under fire – was the same given during the last visit a couple of weeks previously. I asked the commanding officer about the casualties the unit had suffered as a result of the intense artillery bombardments of his positions and was given an answer that was as economical as it was enigmatic – 'few'.

After a few seconds of deliberation, he opened up a little more – 'but I lost two only this morning. Sniper. Whilst one of them was taking a crap.' It was not every day I heard news like that so I asked for more details. Apparently, under the cover of darkness, a Serb sniper must have sneaked into range of the foxhole sheltering the two unfortunate soldiers in question. As the relief team arrived at around noon, they found their comrades lying dead, one with his trousers around his ankles in the middle of his morning ablutions, shot in the head. The other lay a few metres away, probably shot in his attempt to help his friend. I could see the CO did not know whether to laugh or cry as he related this tragi-comic story. The harsh reality of war engenders a basic and unsentimental form of banana skin humour, but he was also aware that the incident that would produce bellows of laughter over drinks in the future also spelled emotional turmoil for the two pairs of devasted parents to whom it was his unpleasant duty to write.

It made me think of those slushy, death-or-glory war films, where the hero sacrifices his life with a steady gaze and jutting chin as he launches a suicidal attack on an enemy that outnumbers him. The real thing is not quite like that. War is tough, raw and sordid. It may bring moments of supreme excitement but the lives of the heroes involved are not always lost in the major offensive that will save king and country but often in banal, almost ridiculous incidents without a trace of the glorious. 'Dear Mrs Smith, it is with the deepest regret that I must write to inform you that your son, John, was killed in action against the Serbs on the morning of bloppety-blop 1993 whilst engaged in a bowel movement.' Not really John Wayne stuff, is it? It does not quite fit in with our preconceptions of war and heroics. Unfortunately, it is the unsentimental truth.

By mid-October, the Maslenica Bridge was losing its status as a 'hot-spot'. It was almost as if the Serbs had accepted its existence and given up arguing about it. Rumblings from the Serb guns were now a rare event, which made life at the OP considerably safer and considerably more dull. And boredom once more became our enemy. This and the strong, biting north-easterly wind known as the Bura, which cut through to the marrow of your bones, or the slightly more merciful and warmer southerly wind, the Jugo, which merely froze your ears, meant our stay here was no longer the pleasant relief from the hectic life of Zadar it had been only six weeks earlier.

On the 25 km drive to and from the OP, I had acquired the habit of counting all the insults and coarse gestures hurled at us along the way by those who were less than enamoured with UNPROFOR. There were more than enough to make the exercise worthwhile. I never made the journey without at least one gesticulation to help me on my way and the record was five – four middle fingers raised vertically and one clenched fist. Not even the Bosnian Serbs demonstrated such collective hostility towards us and they had been on the receiving end of strongly-worded UN sanctions. Even though I had met friendly Croats, our family in Sibenik to name the best example, I had to accept the regrettable conclusion yet again that I was still to see them in their best light. I understood very well their frustration but the way in which it was expressed was not the most likely to make friends.

On 31 October, I discovered that certain Croats still worshipped idols that Croatia officially denies, in circumstances very similar to that day in HVO Military Police headquarters in Mostar. I was patrolling the front line when I came across two vehicles from Cobra Brigade, one of HV's professional units. On the sides of both, there was a large black Maltese cross with a white death-head in the middle. The front bumper of one of the vehicles bore the hand-painted inscription, 'Cobra SS'. If they really wanted to convince the Serbian minority that their rights would be respected in the event of a surrender by Serb troops, such displays would do no good whatsoever, particularly bearing in mind the bloody conflict the two had been through. On the other hand, if the intention was to send a signal to the Serbs that now might be a good time to find somewhere else to live, it was just as good as buying prime time on a satellite television station.

As October drew to a close, another serious effort was made in Sector South to bring about a real ceasefire instead of the sham that had been in force for the past few months. This was the third attempt since I had been posted to the Sector and no efforts were spared to ensure success. Both parties agreed to try once more to bring an end to hostilities. We received extra men, set up new observation posts and manned them round the clock. We now had the entire front line under observation. We worked like dogs and hardly slept at all to stretch our resources to provide surveillance of the enormous area in our sector. It was worth it. Hostilities declined measurably and we wallowed in pride and happiness. But after only a few days, we had to scale down our observation routines to catch up on some sleep. This of course provided opportunities for cheating and cheat they did, so after a couple of weeks although hostilities were still not what they had been, we could not, with our hands on our hearts, claim to have effected a true ceasefire.

On 4 November, I drove from Sector South to the Bihac Pocket in north-west Bosnia-Herzegovina, where I was to spend the last three months of my service. I left with a feeling of having done a job I could be proud of. Peace did not come in the three months I was there but UNPROFOR could not be accused of not trying. A neutral force cannot bring about peace on its own and, all in all, I do not think we could have done more than we did, at least not with the resources we had at our disposal.

*Chapter 10*

# Velika Kladusa –
# In the Kingdom of 'Babo'

T he most important town in the Muslim-controlled pocket is
Bihac, at its southern end. Ten kilometres north-west of the
town, UNPROFOR had established a crossing in the front line
facing the Krajinan Serbs giving access to the pocket, which was
surrounded by Krajina Serbian forces to the north, west and south
and Bosnian Serbs to the east. The front line against the Krajinan
Serbs, a very quiet front, followed the border with Croatia. The
crossing in the front line was established at a long, straight road with
open ground on both sides. As we approached the border of the
republic of Bosnia-Herzegovina, I could see that it was marked by a
number of live anti-tank mines placed on the road in such a way you
had to slalom your vehicle through them, which is exactly what our
driver, a Jordanian lieutenant-colonel, did. The trouble was he did it
at 60 kph on a wet road, a demonstration of driving skills that was
not greatly appreciated by the passengers. I had not been in the Bihac
Pocket for more than two minutes before I saw the first clear indications that I was back in Muslim-controlled territory: minarets,
green flags with white crescent moons, peasant women in baggy
pants and hordes of waving, cheering children. After three months
in Croatia, I was overwhelmed at such open demonstrations of
friendliness but I soon recovered my Mostar approach to people and
life and for the next three months, it was the most natural thing in
the world to offer a daily, friendly greeting as we passed people in the
street.

My team came to pick me up in Bihac – Marian from the Czech
Republic, Sammi from Ghana and Joram from Kenya. Joram was
team leader, a stout, robust little man with the deepest voice I had
ever heard. His stature and habit of speaking in short oompah bursts

122

made him a living caricature of a tuba in military band – an appearance that belied his true self. He was a professional and enthusiastic officer with whom I enjoyed an excellent relationship once we had finished sniffing each other in best meeting-dog fashion.

We quickly took our leave of Bihac and drove to the team's home town of Velika Kladusa in the north-west corner of the pocket. It was only about 40 km away but the drive took well over an hour, mainly because of the twisting and tortuous mountain roads north of Bihac. The rest of the pocket was not mountainous, though decidedly hilly. The long, flat stretches of open ground I knew so well from Denmark were not part of the topology here. During the drive, I was given a briefing on the area and I kept my mouth shut and ears open. Three different front lines, one of which could move kilometres in the course of a single day, a republic that had unilaterally declared independence, two groups of Muslims engaged in an internal struggle, Serbs collaborating with Muslims and Croats supplying Muslims with commercial goods via a trade corridor to Zagreb and acting as bodyguards for a Muslim commander-in-chief. My head was whirling with this confusing state of affairs and I soon realised that the Bihac Pocket was going to be a difficult, though fascinating and challenging, place to work. Things here changed dramatically from day to day. The Bihac Pocket was a hornet's nest and living in it was to keep me more than busy from day one. But first a little background.

Fighting broke out in the Bihac Pocket on 12 June 1992 at 0500, when Serb artillery opened fire on Bihac. A few days later, a full-scale war was being waged and within a month, the front line, as it appeared when I arrived in the area, had been more or less established. An infantry unit was quickly formed to defend the area's territory – strong in numbers but very poorly equipped – known as '5th Corps Armija BiH'. It consisted of eight brigades and an HVO battalion, in all, some 25,000 men. The Corps also boasted an ancient T-55 tank with eight shells, taken from the Bosnian Serbs in the first few days of the war. This single tank represented the Muslim's entire tank reserves.

Communications between Bihac and the central government in Sarajevo were difficult in the extreme and could only be achieved with help from the UN, who moved key personnel from one place to another by helicopter. Supplies were a different matter. They could not be transported from Central Bosnia to the north-west corner which had been left to sort out its own logistics problems,

123

thereby achieving some degree of independence. The Bihac Pocket was represented in the nine-man Bosnian presidential council by Fikret Abdic. Before the war, he had been the long-standing managing director of the foodstuff company, Agrokomers, one of former Yugoslavia's largest and most successful companies. Abdic had brought financial security to the Bihac area and enjoyed the respect of all three population groups, who were more or less equally represented in Agrokomers staff. In his home town of Velika Kladusa, he was very much the local hero. In 1987, Agrokomers had got mixed up in a scandal involving the issuing of forged IOUs. Abdic went to prison but was released after two years because of lack of evidence. This affair had split the people into two camps – was Abdic a villain or a victim? Before the fragmentation of Yugoslavia, he entered the political arena through the Muslim party SDA and is said to have won more votes at the 1990 autumn election than Alija Izetbegovic but conceded victory to him out of respect for his greater political experience and greater breadth of support in parliament.

For some time, there had been increasing tension between Abdic and Izetbegovic over the conditions for making peace with the Croats and Serbs, coming to a head with the Bosnian parliament's rejection of the Geneva Peace Plan of September 1993. This apparently was the last straw that broke the camel's back. On 29 September, Abdic declared himself President of 'AP Zapadna Bosna' (the Autonomous Province of West Bosnia). Now they could dismiss orders from Sarajevo with scorn. Behind this turn of events lay a strong conviction that the war had been going on long enough and must be brought to an end. The Muslims had to face up to the fact that they had lost the war, and the sooner the better if there were to be no more casualties. Shortly afterwards he and Mate Boban[1] signed an agreement in Zagreb of mutual recognition of each others republics. The signatures on the documents were witnessed by President Tudjman. Abdic subsequently came to the same agreement with Radovan Karadic in Belgrade, with the witness this time none less than President Milosevic[2]. As security for his drastic actions, Abdic had committed his support with the northern brigades of the 5th Corps. In a hastily organised campaign, 90% of the 70,000 people of the Velika Kladusa region signed a petition to show their support for Abdic. A similar event was attempted in Cazin, south of Kladusa, only to be nipped in the bud by the local brigade commander.

The declaration of independence seemed not to be the cause of any in-fighting between splinter groups and the majority who had remained loyal to the government in Sarajevo. At least for a few days. Almost inevitably, trouble started and quickly gathered momentum so that there was soon an internal front line. Muslim was now in arms against Muslim, a little reluctantly to start with. After all, this was brother fighting brother. But the bond of brotherhood melted in the heat of the argument and before long, this local skirmish assumed the stature and character of the war with the Bosnian Serbs. The first real civil war in former Yugoslavia had broken out.

To ensure the economic survival of the area, Abdic entered an agreement with Tudjman to make the Bihac Pocket a free trade area with the Croatian coastal town of Rijeka as its free-port. Abdic managed quickly to achieve remarkable results for the people of this self-declared republic. Prisoners were exchanged with the Serbs and goods from Croatia rolled into the country from Krajina, transported in Agrokomers trucks. The goods were sold at controlled prices that were affordable to everyone. In Velika Kladusa, everything was available and everything was on sale, a situation which soon embittered the pocket's remaining 180,000 Muslims in the area under the control of that part of the 5th Corps still loyal to Sarajevo, who were denied every item of luxury goods.

What Abdic had done when he declared independence was an astonishingly audacious move. He freed 80% of the front-line units and repositioned them along the internal front line, now grouped in five brigades – brigades by name only; numerically they were more battalions. He had bet his shirt and was now completely at the mercy of the Serbs. Everything depended on how serious they wanted to sue for peace. This delicate situation created an imbalance between the tiny republic and its large Serbian neighbour. The perception at any rate was clear that Abdic was forced to stand before the Serbs with cap in hand.

The reaction from the government in Sarajevo was brutal and swift. Abdic was declared a traitor who was to be removed immediately. The 5th Corps loyalists agreed – Abdic had sold his birthright to the Serbs for power and personal gain. The perception was that it was not only the shirt off his own back he had bet. He had brought into danger the entire Bihac Pocket, which hundreds of Muslims had died defending. This act of treason was intolerable and if Abdic was unwilling to renounce his actions of autonomy willingly, he would have to be forced to. Abdic rejected the idea out of hand and made it unambiguously clear that he intended to spread his autonomic thinking to the entire Bihac Pocket.

This explains why the fronts were so firmly entrenched when I showed up, just a month after the internal schism, and I laboured under no misapprehensions that both sides would fight for their convictions with a will of steel.

On the international level as well, the declaration of autonomy failed to achieve the breakthrough Abdic had hoped for. Geneva responded by simply not inviting him to continue in the peace negotiations, despite the fact that he had the reputation of being a pragmatic and goal-oriented negotiator. The UN refused formally to accept the independent province but had no alternative but to acknowledge it as a concrete element in the local balance of power. The western press dubbed him as a slightly deranged war-monger who had declared independence for highly doubtful reasons of personal gain.

One of the Gordian knots Abdic managed to unravel was that of Bosanka Bojna, a 25 sq km area on the north-east corner of the Bihac Pocket that had been a regular site of brawls with the Krajinan Serbs. At the outbreak of war, the majority of the population of Bos Bojna, as it was popularly known, had been Serbs but they were quickly driven out. They settled just on the other side of the border and were given every support from their Krajinan Serb cousins to make life as unpleasant as possible for the Muslims who controlled the area. Such action was restricted to irritation until 27 April 1993, when the Serbs launched a full-scale offensive and in the space of a few days had regained most of Bos Bojna. Ever since, the 5th Corps had carried out a continuous programme of minor attacks in an attempt to repossess their lost territory, all of which failed. UNPROFOR had worked hard to pour oil onto troubled waters by getting the area declared a demilitarised zone under UN surveillance. The 5th Corps' response was immediate rejection of any such plan. Bos Bojna, they claimed, was part of Bosnia-Herzegovina, in which the Armija BiH, and therefore 5th Corps, was the army of the official government and they had a legitimate right to be there. The situation was a deadlock until Abdic, shortly after declaring independence, accepted the UN proposal for demilitarisation, to the chagrin and annoyance of the 5th Corps senior officers.

Almost immediately, the plan ran into problems. Nobody could agree in principle on the future status of the area. More practically, it was proving difficult to get the Serbs to honour the agreement and withdraw their weapons. Most of their heavy guns had been removed but their small-arms remained, in flagrant disregard for any promises made. Responsible for ensuring all weapons had actually been removed was the French UN battalion and it is possible they were anxious about a possible confrontation with the Serbs. At any rate, they did not do the job very well. They made such a hash of it, in fact, that Abdic tried to get the much more respected Danish battalion, DANBAT[3], to take over the job, a request which proved impossible to grant as DANBAT's mandate extended only to their insertion in Croatia. When I heard this news, I remember thinking to myself, 'Why don't the Muslims fight fire with fire and move their guns into the demilitarised zone, just like the Serbs?' The answer was given the first time I witnessed a meeting between senior officers from the two sides – the Muslims simply did not feel strong enough to bluff in this high-stakes game. Not only were they utterly dependent on the goods that had to be transported through Serbian territory but they were only too well aware that the province was highly vulnerable to an attack from the rear. The Bos Bojna dilemma was very typical of the relationship between the autonomous province and its mighty Krajinan Serb neighbour. It could only continue to exist with the tacit acceptance of others, and the Serbs made sure they got their pound of flesh. They did exactly what suited them and if the Muslims did not like it, they could lump it.

The date of my arrival in this province, 5 November 1993, was an eagerly awaited Feast Day. Abdic's agreements with the Serbs and Croats opened the borders for friends and family to visit, something which had not been possible for a year and a half. It was on that day that the first three Agrokomers buses would roll in and their arrival was anticipated with great excitement. Thousands of people had gathered at the town square in Velika Kladusa when Joram, our interpreter Jasmina and I arrived at 1600. We had to take the last stretch on foot as it was impossible to park in the square itself. It was as packed as Times Square on New Year's Eve. We made our way to the UNHCR office on the third floor of a building which afforded a grandstand view of the proceedings. In the middle of the square, a stand had been erected, from which a pair of enormous loudspeakers blared out Bosnian folk music that made the chilly autumn air quiver in surprise. At regular intervals, the crowd was informed of the progress of the buses, even though their arrival was not scheduled until 1900. Rain started lancing down but was accepted with impunity by the throng of excited people, growing larger all the time as if in defiance of the very elements.

Every now and then, the music was interrupted by speeches of praise and glory to the man who had made it all possible, Fikret Abdic, known to all as *Babo*[4]. They ended without exception with the crowd chanting in best football fashion, *'Ba-bo, Ba-bo, Ba-bo!'* The legions of soldiers present were also warned not to fire into the air when the buses arrived, for the safety of the crowd. The poor speaker might as well have saved his breath. When the crowd caught the first glimpse of the buses at the end of the main street leading into the square, all hell broke loose. The hysterical masses thronged around them, cheering and shouting in glee. As night follows day, this was met with a fireworks display beyond comparison as automatic rifles began barking their own special *a cappella* welcome, with magazine after magazine being emptied until the muzzles were so hot the bullets traced long, curling tongues of condensation in the cold evening air. It was a sight to behold. The soldiers were ordered by a frantic military policeman to cease firing but he was blithely disobeyed, indeed it is highly unlikely he was even heard by the euphoric people who, for the first time in many months, had something to celebrate. They enjoyed demonstrating their joy with thousands of bullets which, these days, were reserved for bringing death, not pleasure.

It was more by luck than judgement that nobody came to any harm as a result of this carefree discharge of deadly weapons that seemed to be so central to the orgy of uninhibited ecstasy. At the risk of seeming a wet blanket, I should also point out that the Muslims had a serious shortage of ammunition.

Joram and I left the square at about 2300 when the party was many hours from drawing to a close. As we drove back to the house, I felt I had been part of a great experience. I realised I had landed up in quite a special place, where everything could happen, and where dreams could come true. In the kingdom of *Babo*, one of the rules was that nobody knew what the day would bring until the sun had set.

1. Mate Boban was then president of the self-declared Bosnian-Croatian republic 'Herceg Bosna', with Mostar as its capital.
2. Karadic was leader of the self-declared 'Bosnian-Serbian Republic'. Milosevic is the president of Serbia.
3. DANBAT had responsibility for part of Sector North in Serb-controlled Krajina in

Croatia. It was the second time this century that Danes had been in this area. The first time was in 1943, when the volunteer *Waffen-SS* regiment, 'Danmark', part of the 'Nordland' division, fought against Tito's partisans. With their latest visit, Danes were made much more welcome by the Serbian population.

4. *Babo* means 'grandfather' and is colloquially used for someone regarded as protector, patron and patriarch.

## Chapter 11

# *Velika Kladusa – Father Fights Son*

On our first patrol of the front line the morning after my arrival, the party mood from the night's festivities on the main square of Velika Kladusa had evaporated with the morning sun. Out here in the most forward positions, where death was a constant companion reaping, little by little, his gruesome harvest, it had developed into more of a hangover. The situation was not made any more bearable by the fact that the enemy was old comrades in arms, often old friends and, in some pitiful cases, members of the family. The troops were very bitter about the consequences of the declaration of independence, a bitterness that was directed not against *'Babo'*, who commanded the greatest respect among most of them, but against the 5th Corps commanders. It was the unspoken wish of virtually every soldier on both sides to bury the hatchet but until that wish was officially granted, they would continue to kill their own. Time and again I heard them say, 'We have to open fire. The extremists are conning them into firing at us and we have to return their fire.' The epithet 'extremists' was a much-used derogatory term for the commanders and certain units of the 5th Corps, whom the Abdic supporters wanted to see stamped as inflexible fundamentalists, steadfastly refusing to accept any form of compromise with the Serbs and Croats.

Even the internal front line, as shown in the map section, differed from any of the front lines I had seen in other sectors. Along its length, most of the fighting was conducted with hand weapons, supported by the occasional heavy weapon, including mortars. This supporting fire, however, nowhere near reached the scale I had seen in Mostar and Sector South. Defence of this front line was also relatively thin on the ground, for no other reason than the shortage of troops in the Abdic camp. In contrast, the 5th Corps was strong in numbers but unable to re-deploy troops from the tough and manpower-intensive front line against the Bosnian Serbs. The end result was that on the internal front line most of the fighting involved villages and features of strategic importance. At no point along the line, from either side, were there heavy concentrations of troops. This meant that there were, as it were, holes in the wall, through which it was possible to sneak and carry out surprise attacks on the enemy's flank or rear, a tactic often employed by both sides. The weakly defended line also allowed the parties to make attacks deep behind the lines before the opponents, both of whom were poorly equipped with arms and vehicles, were able to reorganise and launch a counter-attack. The danger of such strikes, however, was reduced by the extensive intelligence networks that both sides had successfully established. In the early days of the conflict, the phone lines were still intact, so intelligence reports were simply delivered over the phone. Later on, the warring parties used informers who, could pass through the lines almost unhindered in places.

Just how unpredictable the front line really was became apparent the day after my arrival. We were visiting a brigade commander at his forward command post in the Johovica area in the north-west corner of the pocket. As we approached the area, we stopped on a hilltop to see if there was any fighting. There was not a sound to be heard, apart from a couple of dogs howling somewhere between us and the command post a kilometre or so away, so we continued on our way. The commander received us warmly, as did all the Abdic commanders, and the atmosphere was relaxed and friendly as we navigated our way through the obligatory preliminary small-talk. We asked him what the situation was on his front line and he replied, 'Oh, things are fine enough really. We had to withdraw a bit to establish a better position.' I then asked him where his most forward position in the area was. To my great surprise, he made a quarter turn and said, 'There,' pointing to a cluster of houses about 100 metres up the road. 'But by the way, I've just given orders to fire on an enemy position up there,' he continued, pointing now at a water tower at the top of a hill some 400 metres from the designated target. He had hardly got the words out of his mouth before three 120-mm mortar shells hit the hilltop in quick succession. A few moments later, the fire was returned and a salvo of mortars fell around the command station.

With my lack of knowledge of the local tactical situation, I was completely confused. Here I was, enjoying a cosy chat about this and that, wearing neither flak jacket nor helmet, and suddenly I found myself sitting behind the front line right bang next to a command post that was an obvious target for the mortars. I dashed out to the car to get the two protective items I felt so naked without to the accompaniment of exploding mortar shells on both sides of the line. 'What the hell is going on here? How close are those heavy weapons? Do they know you have your command post here?' A barrage of questions was directed at the brigade commander with rapid fire. Our interpreter, Jasmina, who was far from happy with the situation, was having difficulty concentrating on her translation so his answer did not provide the briefing I needed of this uncomfortable situation. It seemed as though the light had dawned on him that perhaps this was not the best place to hang around and we removed ourselves to a nearby two-storey house to continue our observation of the action. After a while it came to an end and we left the house – and the area.

The incident was another excellent illustration of the fact that the most unpleasant thing in a dangerous situation is not always the danger itself but the uncertainty of its scope and extent. It also served to remind me that in the future we had better equip ourselves with more up-to-date information about the current location of the front line. The others agreed and we decided that from that day forward we would make more thorough observation of a front line area before we made a move towards it. We would also make sure that we obtained the latest information about front line locations from the highest military sources in Velika Kladusa so that we knew precisely how far we could drive without 'crossing the line'.

Late that afternoon, we had just arrived at our house on a hilltop on the outskirts of Velika Kladusa when we received a phone call from the military HQ. They asked us to come immediately as they had important information for us.

The HQ had been set up in a former Agrokomers factory building on the southern outskirts of town. Not far from this factory was the 'presidential palace' – Fikret Abic's residence. It too was located in one of the company's numerous buildings. The team had an excellent, not to say unique, relationship with the military headquarters. We could drop in at will, without any appointment. If there was any staff officer present, we were granted every facility to talk to him. In return, they expected us to be available whenever we were needed, whatever the time of day or night. All in all, it meant we were able to work very effectively within the restraints of our mandate. First and foremost, that involved sending reports of the military situation to the UN hierarchy. In addition, we were tasked with sundry jobs, large and small, including the investigation of the many reports of attack on the civilian population, who were, at regular intervals, made party to the fighting near the highly mobile front line.

The HQ was a curious mixture of civilian and military, men and women, and young and old. Some appeared to be very busy others seemed to have difficulty in passing the time. The entire building, which was heated only by a few paraffin stoves, was permeated with the heavy odour of cabbage from the cellar kitchens. The commander's office was furnished just as spartanly as the one I had seen in Mostar – an old desk, four threadbare armchairs, a wooden-slatted bed, a bookcase, a lamp with no shade and the Bosnian coat of arms. That is as much as was provided for Asim Delic, commander of the massed forces in the autonomous province.

'Please take a seat. The commander is on his way,' said the secretary, who brought us three *kaffa*, the local variety of Turkish coffee.

Delic was a small, scrawny man with a pronounced stoop. He was in his late fifties and had a limp handshake and a tired but friendly face. Hardly what I had imagined of a supreme commander. It did not take long to discover he was a warm and obliging person, for whom this war was a plague which he, more than anyone else, wanted to bring to an end as soon as possible. Our almost daily meet-ings confirmed this impression. He was convinced that immediate peace with the Serbs was the only sensible course of action, a peace which he was equally sure they would respect, so that the Muslim population could also lead a tolerable existence. The senior officers of the 5th Corps, however, stated that he and the others who believed in this salvation were hopelessly naive. Which was, of course, a possibility, depending entirely on the true motives for peace of the Serbs and Croats. But Delic was fighting with a true conviction that peace should be made with the Serbs here and now rather than allowing the war to continue indefinitely. In fact, it was a conviction that was shared by most of the people in the province. They blamed Sarajevo for the fact that the war was still being waged, claiming that the government, with Alija Izetbegovic as its leader, was adamant that Bosnia-Herzegovina retain its sovereignty as a single state.

'Let's get down to business,' said Delic, after we had chatted idly for a while. Early that same morning, a commando unit from the 5th Corps, known as 'Hamze'[1], had infiltrated many kilometres behind the front line and attacked the village of Ponjevici. It was believed to have gone on the rampage and looted the village before withdrawing in the afternoon with 65 civilians whom Delic feared would be used as hostages. He concluded his story by saying that 'Hamze' was from 505 Brigade, based in Buzim and that its troops were 'the worst extremists of them all' and anything could be expected of them. He was in the process of drafting a formal protest over their conduct to be delivered to 5th Corps with UNPROFOR as witness. This, of course, is what we had been summoned for and Delic informed us that he wanted us to drive to Ponjevici the next morning to confirm the intelligence he had received.

We were more than prepared to do this but with the events of that morning still fresh in our memories we asked Delic whether the 'Hamze' raid could have produced any changes to the front-line situation, which he vehemently denied. The most forward units, he reassured us, were still some three kilometres from Ponjevici, so we could set out with no worries.

The next morning we visited Delic once again. He had finalised his protest but it was clear it was the first time he had written such a document. There were several serious omissions. The 65 civilians were not mentioned explicitly, so it had to be re-written if it was to be of any real validity. It may sound curious that it was addressed to the 5th Corps, who in all probability knew what had been going on anyway. They were really only *pro forma* addressee, with the true intention of informing the upper echelons of the UN. This was a tactic in widespread practice throughout former Yugoslavia, where protests against sundry violations of ceasefires and human rights were sent by the truckload via the UN. All warring parties were well aware that their protests would have no effect whatsoever on the behaviour of their opponents and nobody would have wasted the time writing them if it were not for the fact that they were seen by a neutral party.

After meeting Delic, we drove to the village of Todorovo. At the village school, now requisitioned as Military HQ, we met the local brigade commander who was to show us the destruction that had been meted out on Ponjevici. It was less than five kilometres to Ponjevici but as we were in undeveloped farmland, where the only physical links between villages were twisting cattle paths and muddy woodland tracks between the steep hills, it took some considerable time to get there. At one point, the brigade commander asked us to stop at a mosque to check on new developments.

We halted on the crest of a hill, with Ponjevici only a kilometre down the valley. The commander exchanged a few words with the soldiers outside the mosque and then asked us to set off again. The situation remained unchanged. We continued down the hillside and, just before we entered the village, passed a group of about 30 men, lying in pairs behind small hillocks with their weapons at the ready. 'What the hell would a squad of infantry be doing here, three kilometres behind the front line?' I asked myself. As if by telepathy, Joram's deep voice bellowed, 'What the devil is going on? They're taking cover!' as he pointed to a couple of women 100 metres in front of us frantically throwing themselves to the ground behind the wall of a house. The next instant, we heard the whizz of bullets before they smashed into the walls nearby. We turned as one to the brigade commander but he was sitting paralysed from shock and no answer to our unspoken question was forthcoming. Quite what the others in the car were feeling at that instant in time, God alone knows. If they were going through the same torture as me, their minds would be whirring with a thousand thoughts at the same time. I felt utterly confused, sitting in a car with bullets flying around our ears, without so much as helmet or flak jacket to afford some meagre form of protection. They were all in the boot. Why not? The front line was a long way away.

As none of us had the faintest idea of what was going on, including where the fire was coming from, and as the brigade commander was incapable of taking any action, we had to take charge ourselves. We had to get out, and fast. It did not take a military genius to recognise we had been caught in crossfire. A couple of hundred metres to our left there was a steep rise in the middle of the village. We went for it, accelerating impressively and sending small stones clattering in the wheel arches and found cover at the bottom of the rise in a small farmhouse. We had been very quick-witted – or perhaps just lucky. At any rate, we had taken the right direction out of the crossfire and the house was not a target.

When we had gathered our wits, we turned on the noble brigade commander for an explanation. He had now gathered enough composure to give some sort of answer but could offer no explanation and was obviously just as taken aback as we were. In the back of the house, we found a group of ten or so women and children, scared out of their wits and huddling in a corner. Their fear and despair was frozen on their faces like a mask of terror as they screamed for comfort and reassurance. Neither of which we were really capable of giving. One of the women said that the firing only started when we entered the village, which did nothing to improve our foul mood. BOOOOM! We collided into each other as a mortar shell landed 300 metres away, not far from the mosque. Shortly afterwards, there was another, and another – but we could not see where they fell. Now an anti-aircraft gun had begun shelling the houses on the small rise just in front of us. They were using HE rounds (high explosive shells) so when a salvo hit its target, there was a rapid series of loud, sharp explosions. Another brace of mortar shells exploded, closer by the sound of it but we still had no idea where they were falling.

'Is there a back road out of this village?' we asked the brigade commander, who once again was unable to give a definitive answer. The women said there was not. The only way in – or out – of the village was by the road we had arrived on.

We thought about getting on the radio and trying to get a UNMO team from the other side of the internal front line to contact 505 Brigade and tell them to cease fire but quickly dropped the idea. It would take a long time, if it could be done at all, and time was not exactly what we had plenty of, with mortar shells falling like rain. BOOOM! Another mortar shell, then another – this one close to the mosque. They were getting closer. We looked at each other and nodded in agreement that there was only one thing to do – apart from remaining passive and allowing fate to take its course. We had to grit our teeth, hope for the best and drive through the crossfire again, drive as we had never driven before. The decision was far from easy but infinitely more attractive than the alternative.

It was an unbelievably agonising feeling to know that whatever we did we would be putting ourselves at extreme risk. As we stood hunched in the doorway, each waiting for the other to take the initiative, sprint out to the car and get it started, I am sure we all had the same sinking feeling in the pit of our stomachs as someone playing Russian roulette just before he pulls the trigger. Normally, I did not exactly envy the soldiers in the most forward positions but at that moment, I would have traded places with any one of them. What I most wanted to do was toss away my blue helmet, abandon our white car and jump into a foxhole, which gave at least some protection. What we had to do was drive out – and drive like hell. There was nothing else we could do. Another two mortar shells falling close by reminded us that we had to get out NOW! At the same moment, we saw a man running down the hillside in front of us. He had emerged from one of the houses that had been battered by the AA gun for the last few minutes. He had taken as much as he could stand and was fleeing from that inferno towards us. He reached the bottom just as we were about to let the clutch out and seeing we were about to run the gauntlet of the crossfire, he made this astonishing statement: 'Why don't you take the back road?'

'Back road? What back road?' But it was true. Wonderfully, gloriously true. Four hundred metres away there was a narrow cattle track up through the woods leading away from this hellhole. We found it. Such as it was. Steep and an absolute quagmire. but we were not that fussy. To us, faced with the alternative of racing through the crossfire, it was the Yellow Brick Road that led to Oz. We were none too happy about leaving those terrified people but there was nothing, absolutely nothing, we could do to bring an end to the madness. And there was, I confess, a limit to the danger we were prepared to accept on their behalf. We had come here to help them, not to get killed. This was one of those nasty situations where we put our own safety first.

The car made it and soon we were out of harm's way. We stopped the car, got out, looked at each other and burst into laughter. A weird reaction but at the time, it seemed the right thing to do. We were overjoyed at having got out unscathed. I looked at my watch. It said 1200, 11 November 1993. The whole incident, from seeing those prostrate soldiers until nervous laughter, had taken slightly less than an hour. I felt considerably more than an hour older.

We drove back to Asim Delic, confident he would have a plausible explanation of how, for all his reassurances, we could have ended up as the targets in a turkey shoot. Alack and alas – he was despondent in his apologies and cursed the recurring problems with communication. That did not go far in pacifying us and for the first and only time, I felt more than justified in feeling let down and angry at this otherwise friendly man. In fact, highly pissed off. A few days later the brigade commander was relieved, which seemed an eminently sensible decision. It was yet another lesson in how extraordinarily mobile this front line could be. A lesson, too, that in future we would rely *solely* on information we had gathered *ourselves*. Apparently, even military commanders were not always correctly informed about the situation in their own area, which was a sorry indication of their professionalism. I never saw such a glaring example again but got the overall impression that most of the military commanders in the autonomous province were more amiable than able.

In the sector that covered the Bihac Pocket, we held a weekly meeting at the HQ in Bihac itself. We always used the main road running north-south, which meant we had to cross the internal front line at the village of Skokovi on top of a ridge which granted a panoramic view of the area. Skokovi was the key position in the area. He who conquered this ridge stood at the portals of the entire province. Both sides knew this and were not mean in the use of resources in their efforts to gain control of the area. The result was daily confrontation, either in the form of orthodox infantry action or bilateral mortar attacks. Skokovi was in the hands of the forces of the autonomous province and had been since the beginning of the conflict.

The French UN battalion had two APCs on task 4 km north and south of the village, ready to escort vehicles over the front line, which in this sector followed steep and meandering mountain roads, often wet and slippery. All of which meant that speeds had to be kept low, and with an APC at the van, even lower. The slow pace was of no concern for the soldiers tucked away inside the APC. They were safe and snug behind armour plate. But for us, in our pathetically wafer-thin car, we needed to be able to accelerate our way out of trouble. For this very sensible reason, we always tried to cross without an escort – to the horror of the French who had the last word in the matter and stopped us every time. So we tried to make our crossing in the APC but this presented problems as well. How would we make our way to Bihac? Fair question. So it ended up with us crossing in convoy, clad in flak jacket, helmet and with fingers and toes crossed. On the stretch of road separating the two opponents there were several places where the mountainside was almost sheer, which presented an extra hazard when snow began to fall. But the most awful thing about this road was the feeling of desolation and emptiness across the 1,000 metres that separated the two parties. It was as if all forms of life had disappeared from the face of the earth, which made the occasional mortar shell, as the only sign of the presence of life, even more vivid.

A sniper hardly needed to be a marksman to take out a soldier in a UN vehicle transiting this stretch of road. And it was this ever-present risk that gave me, from the very first time, the chilling sensation in my spine that I could well be today's sitting duck for those 'soldiers' who refused to accept that UN forces were not a legitimate target. You could, of course, be shot at by snipers anywhere and everywhere behind the front line but, funnily enough, it was only on this stretch of road that I ever got this uncomfortable feeling. I believe this stems from my experiences in Mostar, where I learned that the atmosphere on the front line itself was very different from the mood behind it. On the front line, emotions are stretched, if you are not careful, you can die. The anguish and bitterness at losing a friend are magnified and immediate. This dangerous cocktail of strong emotions was the fuse to a powder keg and we paid it the greatest respect, particularly when crossing the front line in unarmoured vehicles, even in convoy. So it was very much against my better judgement that we crossed the front line at Skokovi in our patrol car.

There was another way of getting to Bihac – through Krajina, but it put another hour on the journey and I was the only one who seemed to think the delay worthwhile. I felt, right down to my bones, that all this criss-crossing over an active front line was tempting fate more than a little. My real problem was that up to now, I could only base my fears on intuition and not concrete evidence of incidents in this sector, which so far had not seen any blatant attacks on UN soldiers. I had no choice but to accept, albeit reluctantly, that we would continue to pass through Skokovi, and the nearby moonscape, on our way to Bihac.

Winter set in very early that year. On the morning of 13 November, the whole area was blanketed with 30 cm of crisp, new-fallen snow. Joram, usually so solemn and serious, was as delighted as a toddler. It was the first time in his 35 years that he had seen snow. He cavorted about in it, making snowballs and constantly shrieking, 'Oooh, it's very cold!' When Sammi from Ghana waddled through the door swathed in seven layers of clothing, he looked for all the world like a Japanese sumo wrestler and it was not easy job to persuade him that if he did not want to freeze to death outside, he had to shed some of those layers. I had to teach them the most elementary things about life in winter, such as banging the snow off their boots at regular intervals to avoid getting wet feet. But in all fairness, where should they have learned such things? The icy roads also gave them real problems, especially Sammi, who was scared to death of skidding over the edge of the precipice and at all times avoided his spell as driver.

The snow imposed an extra hardship on the front-line soldiers. Up to now, they had been able to concentrate on killing each other, but now the weather was making them think more about survival than destruction. Temperatures were already varying from +5°C in daytime to –10°C at night. This swing meant the landscape was one giant field of slush during the day and an expanse of hard, slippery concrete at night, unless there was a new fall of snow, which there invariably was. Even well-trained and well-equipped soldiers laboured under the change in weather and how the ill-equipped Muslim soldiers managed is something which still earns my admiration. Most seriously, only a very few possessed a decent pair of military boots. Most had to make do with what they had when they put on 'uniform', usually woollen socks and a pair of casual shoes or trainers. Uniform was worn by about half of them, with the remainder dressed in a motley ragbag of plain clothes with the colours of the coat of Joseph's dream. Even the ones in uniform did not look much smarter or more warlike. There were two models of uniform, both home-made and of varying design. The most up-market model was made of reasonably heavy-duty camouflage canvas which was adequate enough. The other was made of thin, beige camouflage material. For the life of me, I could not imagine what it had possibly been used for before the war. It looked more like a pair of grandad's old pyjamas. Very few wore headgear and none had a helmet. I felt desperately sorry for these ragamuffin soldiers when I saw them shambling and shuffling their way through the slush on their way to the skating rink that was their front line by night. Inevitably, not more than a week passed before we heard of the first cases of casualties to frostbite and exposure.

One morning less than ten days after the first snow, we saw the first 'strange phenomena' in the form of Muslim soldiers in black leather boots and crisp new Croatian camouflage uniforms. Abdic had been on a shopping spree to his 'friends' in Zagreb and was now dressing his army for winter. Over the next two weeks, the rags turned to britches and morale was boosted – for a while at least. Before long, the occasional uniform was seen among the soldiers of the 5th Corps. They had been taken from captured Abdic soldiers and had the status and prestige of priceless scalps.

The import of uniforms in bulk to the province naturally raised the question of whether military hardware was finding its way in the same shipments, which would have been a clear violation of the UN embargo. Checking the stream of trucks that passed the various checkpoints between Krajina and the autonomous province was the job of the French UN contingent. We were to keep our eyes peeled for heavy support weapons. These were seldom seen but new automatic rifles were commonplace. There was no doubt that Abdic was bringing weapons in from Croatia through Serb-controlled Krajina.

I had the distinct impression that the checks made by the French were far from effective, but even if they had been, there were dozens of trails that could have been used by the illicit convoys. The situation gave me a much better understanding of the problems inherent in an arms embargo, which is a sanction that is very simple to institute and unbelievably difficult and resource-consuming to enforce.

During our daily patrols, we regularly assisted the UNHCR in visiting local families to ensure that the UN food supplies were reaching the civilian population as intended. It was a task that led us near and far, from families in Velika Kladusa to families in the most remote and isolated hamlets, apparently out of touch with the modern world. It was these visits that were the most interesting as we glimpsed a lifestyle that I, for one, had never imagined possible. Many of these families, usually of three generations, lived in tiny, primitive hovels with no modern conveniences. Almost all of them were overrun with children, which was hardly surprising when most of the girls started producing them at 18. They stared in amazement when I told them that, at the ripe old age of 28, I had still not become a father. The families were more or less self-sufficient, with their little plots of land and a few animals. What they could not produce themselves they obtained by barter. The inside of the cottages was generally one large single room occupied by the entire family. This was where all the domestic chores were done, from preparing food to washing sweaty socks. It was rarely less than 30°C in these rooms and as warmth is a precious commodity and not to be squandered by opening windows, the air was stale and heavy. It always took a few minutes for the nose to acclimatise to the exotic atmosphere and returning to the fresh air of rural Bosnia was like taking a cold shower after a sweltering sauna. But what these people lacked in hygiene they more than made up for in hospitality and generosity of spirit. However poor they seemed, we never visited any family without being offered food and coffee.

It was our overall impression that food supplies were getting through effectively, even to the most remote villages. The army took some but they too had mouths to feed. Blatant abuse of the aid at the expense of their own civilian population was rarely seen. Abuse at the expense of the civilian population of the enemy, however, was something we saw all too often practised by the overlords of the autonomous province. The usual food aid route was from Zagreb to Velika Kladusa and onwards to Bihac. Often, the convoys were denied passage across the internal front line on the flimsiest of excuses, all founded on the unsympathetic reluctance to allow the food to get to areas where it was desperately needed. It was all too apparent that the autonomous province was using the food aid as a weapon directed against the 5th Corps. The intention was to starve the civilian population into rebelling against the leaders of the 5th Corps so that the entire Bihac Pocket would fall into autonomous hands. Escorting the convoys across the internal front line was the lot of the French who, on one occasion, became so incensed at being refused free passage yet again that they threatened to shoot their way through. Bluff or not, it paid off and within a few hours the convoy was on its way to Bihac. The orders to practise these tactics must have come from a high ranking official in the 'government' of the autonomous province. My personal opinion is that it was Abdic himself.

In all the time I spent in the province, I only met Abdic on one occasion and then only because we were accompanying the Dutch General Bastiaans, Supreme Commander of all Military Observers in former Yugoslavia. Abdic was desperately trying to establish the status of statesman, on a par with the other recognised self-declared leaders in the war-torn country. Part of this strategy was his outright refusal to meet the commander of the 5th Corps to discuss conditions for peace. Matters of such importance he would only discuss with Alija Izetbegovic himself. Abdic was a small, stocky very voluble man, very dynamic and determined, but evidently under the strain of the enormous responsibility that rested on his shoulders. Despite his presumed guilt in stopping the food supplies to Bihac he made a fairly positive impression, even with his tendency to self-importance and blind conviction of the right of his opinions. The most notable thing he said during the meeting was that the final goal of the autonomous province was that it should include the entire Bihac Pocket. Whether that would be achieved peaceably or by force was entirely up to Izetbegovic. It was plain speaking indeed, and as Izetbegovic believed Abdic to be guilty of high treason it was obvious to me from then on that this internal struggle could well run the full course.

In a way, this realisation was disillusioning. We were here for the express purpose of helping them towards a peaceful solution. On the other hand, I had accepted in the early days in Mostar that the UN, as a neutral party, could not impose any conditions that the conflicting parties were not willing to accept. So once again I had to wrestle with the depressing thought that I would have to go on working hard, often in dangerous situations, for something I knew was almost doomed to failure from the start. If I had gone to former Yugoslavia out of pure idealism, such a conclusion would have been impossible to live with, so I found solace in the fact that I had also made the journey partly for the experience and adventure alone. That meant I could still put all my energy into the job without being disappointed and depressed when it failed. I was learning to regard all the difficulties and downright fiascos as unique and invaluable experiences.

On 15 November, we received information that the 5th Corps had attacked the village of Todorovo that very morning and that the fighting was still fierce. We modified our patrol plan and drove immediately to the village to confirm our information. Ten kilometres south of Velika Kladusa, we saw the first indications that something serious had happened. Straggling groups of women, children and old people were on the road, bent under the weight of bags, sacks and miscellaneous belongings from their homes. We stopped an open truck to hear what had happened. The driver told us that the Corps had indeed attacked Todorovo and that the civilian population was fleeing not only from that village but the whole area to the south, fearing that the attack would continue and cut off their only route of escape. An old women was sitting in the cab, looking at us with lips compressed to thin lines in her fight to contain the tears that were welling in her eyes. In the back of the truck, there were more people, some quaking with fear, others staring dispassionately into space, close to a state of apathy. We moved on, passing group after group of refugees until we arrived at the junction to Todorovo. Here we encountered a group of about 30 men, busy emptying ammunition boxes. Many were past the age normally considered fit for military service. But soldiers were in short supply, so it was all hands to the pumps, including men who could well be grandfathers. We continued up the road towards Todorovo but stopped a kilometre short of town as the battle was still raging furiously. We stayed and observed for an hour or so whilst the shooting droned on, spiced at regular intervals by mortar fire.

When we got back to the main road, reinforcements had arrived, waiting to be sent into the fray with a counter-attack. They were all 20–40 years old and I passed the time of day with them through our interpreter. There was no evidence of fear amongst this group of men, even though they were well aware that the impending battle would be the last for some. In fact, they were in fine fettle and even tried to auction off my boots which they all thought were *'vrlo dobro'* (very fine). After a while orders were given for them to climb aboard the waiting trucks and off they went into the slush and biting cold to an unknown fate in Todorovo. We waved them a *'sretno'* farewell (good luck) which was acknowledged with a cheery *'hvala'* (thank you). Half an hour later, all hell broke loose with a cacophony of mortar shell explosions and machine-gun fire. The counter-offensive was under way. The infernal din continued until the afternoon, when we drove back to Kladusa to send our daily sitrep.

Not until the next afternoon did we get a chance to talk to Asim Delic, who looked a hundred years old, exhausted, unshaven and with sunken eyes. Madness was still raging in Todorovo. The counter-attack had failed with heavy losses being sustained, and as if that were not enough, the most able military commander in the province, Fikret Keserovic, had been taken prisoner during the attack. We knew him well. He was a man of about 45 with closely-cropped steel grey hair, sharp features and ice-blue eyes. He was always to be found where the action was hottest and yet always appeared calm and collected, hence the nickname we had given him – Action Man. Just the day before his capture, Abdic told us, he had assumed command of the Todorovo brigade, taking over from the shell-shocked man who had accompanied us to Ponjevici five days earlier. Keserovic had been appointed with the specific objective of achieving a much needed push at this important sector of the front and regaining the ground lost over the past few weeks. But it was not to be and now he was a PoW in Bihac. Delic went on to tell us the tragic news that it was without a shadow of a doubt that Todorovo's quick fall was due to an act of betrayal. One of the senior officers had betrayed the rest of the staff and effectively annihilated the brigade's internal defences. When he had finished, Delic looked down at his desk and slowly shook his head. He glanced up at us with a crooked smile and, typical of his warm personality, said, 'We will all do anything for our wives. His wife lives in Buzim (in 5th Corps territory) but if my wife were to ask of me what she asked of him, I would refuse.' After a short pause, he went on, 'What he has done, he will have to answer to his conscience for.'

Betrayal was a problem that plagued both sides of the internal front line and was explained by the fact that the breakdown of the 5th Corps had happened by brigades, led by the senior officers. The troops, who wanted none of it, were faced with a problem which they

solved in a variety of ways, from half-hearted acceptance to deser-
tion and treachery.

The battle for Todorovo waged back and forth for weeks with
frequent, though inconclusive, counter-attacks from the Abdic side.
Gradually, however, the leaders of the autonomous province came
to accept that the battle was lost, at least for the time being, and it
grew into a war of position as the days passed. The 5th Corps had
managed to push the Abdic forces six kilometres back along this
front, which meant that the strategically important Skokovi ridge was
now more vulnerable than ever.

A couple of days after the fall of Todorovo, rumours started flying
that the area around the village of Vrnograc to the north-east was
also under threat of attack by the 5th Corps. This was another area
whose loss would be critical as it lay immediately south of the demilitarised zone, Bos Bojna. If the Corps got too close to this area, it
was entirely possible that Krajinan Serbs would attempt to re-occupy
the zone with subsequent loss of face for Abdic. We drove to the
headquarters of the brigade currently holding this section of the front
line to verify the rumours.

In front of the HQ, two royal blue Mercedes 190s were parked,
which Joram told me belonged to Asim Delic. Next to one of them,
stood four young men, who by their appearance must have come
from the more professional units of the province's forces. They were
part of Delic's bodyguard that I had not previously met. It was
perfectly natural for the senior commander of the province's forces
to have a bodyguard as the infiltration of the front line was a regular
occurrence by both sides and it was a fair assumption that there were
numerous fifth columnists. What surprised me about these soldiers
was the small shield-shaped metal badge with a red and white check-
ered design they wore on their chests. It was the coat of arms of the
first king of Croatia, Tomislav[2], worn by all Croatian soldiers. But
what place did such an emblem have here in the Bihac Pocket? To
my amazement, it turned out that Croatian HVO soldiers really had
been given the prestigious task of forming a bodyguard for Delic. So
while Muslims in other parts of Bosnia-Herzegovina were fighting a
bloody war against the Croats, here in the autonomous province they
put their supreme commander's life in the hands of their 'enemy'!

I needed an explanation for this bizarre state of affairs and
Jasmina, our interpreter who had worked for the UNMOs since the
outbreak of war and therefore had an impressive knowledge of
recent local history, was able to provide me with one. When the war

in Bosnia-Herzegovina broke out, the Bihac Pocket had a Croat minority that formed an HVO battalion. It came under the 5th Corps with one company stationed in Velika Kladusa and the rest of the battalion in Bihac. When war broke out between the Croats and Muslims in May 1993, the alliance remained intact in the Bihac Pocket, most probably because the Croats, very much in the minority, had no choice.

With the declaration of the autonomous province and the ensuing internal struggle, the Croats found themselves in a very difficult situation. Partly because they would not fight each other and partly because they regarded the problem as an internal Muslim rebellion, towards which they wanted to maintain a neutral position. This was a position acceptable to both sides who did not, therefore, deploy their respective HVO units on the internal front line. As far as the 5th Corps was concerned, it meant no change – they were still fighting a bloody war against the Bosnian Serbs, which the HVO simply continued to take part in. But the autonomous province had just made peace with both the Bosnian Serbs and the Krajinan Serbs, which meant they had to find new work for the redundant HVO soldiers. A new job that was nothing less than the bodyguard for the supreme military commander of the province. To make everything even more difficult to understand, the company in Kladusa still came under the battalion in Bihac – however they managed to live with that situation in practice. Of all the strange events I experienced in former Yugoslavia, this was one of the most bizarre.

Inside HQ, Delic was in a meeting with the local brigade commander and did not want our participation. We bided the time by talking to the brigade chief of staff, Hasan, a funny fellow with wide-open eyes and round mouth which gave a look of eternal surprise. Like many of the soldiers we met, Hasan got through three packs of cigarettes a day, drank his fair share of booze and got far too little sleep. A lifestyle like that, combined with the stress of being at war, quickly makes its mark and he looked ten years older than he really was. As he had nothing of great importance to tell us, the conversation moved on to other things that had happened in the area. He told us of two of his soldiers who had found themselves in a particularly dreadful situation. They were father and son, both in the deepest of positions against the 505 Buzim Brigade of the 5th Corps, whose most forward positions were only a few hundred metres away. The man's other son was serving with 505 Brigade. The story gave me gooseflesh. Father fights son and son fights brother.

One of the most awful situations imaginable. And it was not the only such case I came across. Later I was to meet others in the same situation and seldom have I met such frustrated and unhappy people.

Our conversation was interrupted by Delic, whose meetings with the brigade commander had come to an end. He told us that he had confirmed intelligence that the 5th Corps was using women and children in Todorovo as shields, preventing Abdic's soldiers from attacking. He asked for our help in organising an evacuation of all women and children with the assistance of the French battalion. This would, of course, require their approval and consent and we promised to talk to them the very next morning. A man of about 40 I would guess, who had been sitting silently and timidly in a corner came over to the table. He was slumped, a trembling nervous wreck on the very edge of a breakdown. He was pale and unshaven with a distant, almost apathetic expression on his face and a handshake as warm and firm as a piece of wet fish. He was obviously in a bad state, which was hardly surprising when we learned that his wife and daughter were among those unfortunates being used as living armour of flesh and blood in Todorovo. He made a desperate appeal for help and we promised we would do everything in our power. But it was not enough to quell his fears. 'But when? When will you help me?' he persisted. We calmed him somewhat by telling him that until a ceasefire had been arranged, so that we and the French could intervene, there was only one thing to be done – to hope and pray for the goodwill and decent human behaviour of the 5th Corps. He had hoped against hope for a more concrete answer but that was the only one we could give. And as useless as it was to him, it was at least honest. He was never to see his family again. Two weeks later 505 Brigade attacked an advanced command post. He was shot in the back by his own comrades. (According to 5th Corps, as he attempted to surrender.) He was but one of untold souls who met their sorry fates in the area.

The day after the meeting, as agreed we made contact with the 5th Corps through the UNMOs in Bihac. After a day's consideration, the Corps commander declared himself willing to enter a ceasefire that was to cover not merely Todorovo but the whole internal front line. Everything possible was done to make the most of this chance and whilst our SMO and the French battalion commander planned the implementation of the ceasefire, we conveyed, with enormous pleasure and surprise, the Corp's answer to Delic. He became equally ecstatic and promised to inform Abdic immediately. It was a much-saddened Delic who informed us the next day that the autonomous province was not interested in a general ceasefire but one that was limited in time and geography, to be effective only in Todorovo, and then only until the civilian population had been evacuated. I could read in his eyes that privately he thought Abdic's decision was madness but he had to maintain a front for us. The answer, which was indeed extraordinary, indicated that despite his defeat at Todorovo he still believed in the military potential of the province and still expected to beat the Corps on the battlefield. To us, as UNMOs, it was an act of insanity that demonstrated how badly Abdic overestimated the military capabilities of the province. What lay behind it we could only guess. One possibility was that he was reckoning with the increased support of the Krajinan Serbs, who were already bombarding the 5th Corps with artillery as a precursor to an Abdic infantry attack. At any rate, from that moment on I regarded Abdic as just as incapable of compromise as he himself accused the 5th Corps of being. It was patently obvious that the internal struggle would continue to the bitter end and with the complete defeat of one of the parties. A peaceful solution now seemed quite unattainable, but it was what we had to go on working for.

Although things looked gloomy in Todorovo, the autonomous province had victories to celebrate elsewhere. At the western end of the front line the Abdic forces were doing extremely well, with new progress being reported almost daily. As we saw the brigade's advanced command post moving further and further south, we assumed this to be true. It was in this area in early November that we had been caught with our pants down. Overnight, the front line was pushed back to a bare 100 metres from the command post. That was now a month ago and in the meantime the brigade had advanced 4–5 kilometres to the edge of the village of Sturlic, the site of bitter fighting the week before. On the morning of 4 December, the command post was pushed forward again, this time into the village itself. It was taken and the event duly celebrated. We saw countless soldiers drunk as skunks, staggering about with a bottle of *slivovic* in one hand and their weapon in the other, emptying magazine after magazine into the air or over a rooftop, depending on the depth of stagger as the trigger was squeezed. If it had not been for the mortal danger to be in the same village as these men, we would probably have stayed longer to enjoy these 'slivo-salvoes' they delighted in as part of their celebration.

What really filled the sails of the Abdic forces on this section of the front line stemmed from a bizarre event that had taken place three days earlier. On 1 December, the UNMO team on the Krajina Serb side of the front line observed three Agrokomers buses, jampacked with armed soldiers in Croatian uniform. With a Serbian military escort, they were making their way south from the town of Slunj, 20 km south-west of Velika Kladusa. We were called on the radio to hear if we had any ideas what it was all about. We did not – but we soon found out. That same afternoon we learned from our colleagues on the 5th Corps side that Abdic forces had just attacked the Corps from the rear to the south of Trzac, which itself was eight kilometres south of Sturlic. It was the latest in a seemingly endless series of surprises in this war in which everything seemed possible. Now Abdic had been given permission to use Krajina as a launch platform for an attack, the clearest demonstration to date of Serbian support for Abdic. It must have come as quite a shock for the 5th Corps soldiers to feel the onslaught of an attack from Krajina, and by Muslim soldiers at that. The lightning strike, coming from all flanks, ended with the Corps losing the entire area between Trzac and Sturlic.

During the attack, Abdic forces were guilty of blatant abuse of UNPROFOR by delivering their wounded to a UN observation post, against every rule of conduct. The UN battalion in question was thus left with two choices – they could either let them die slowly or they could transport them to the hospital in Velika Kladusa. They chose the second option but whether Abdic was later sanctioned, I know not.

The 5th Corps commanders were highly resentful of the fact that UNPROFOR forces in Krajina had not stopped the buses before the Abdic troops were able to launch an attack. And let there be no doubt that that is precisely what should have happened, had we but known their true intentions. Personally, I do not believe the thought crossed anyone's minds until it was a *fait accompli*. It is also a question of whether the UN could have predicted such an unorthodox move. The outcome was that the UN instituted an immediate stepping up of border control between the autonomous province and Krajina to make sure nothing of the sort would ever happen again. But the incident does serve as an excellent illustration of how UNPROFOR functioned. The shenanigans of the warring parties put UNPROFOR on the defensive rather than the offensive, which gave them, rather than UNPROFOR, the initiative, which was hardly the way things were supposed to be. Basically, I believe this situation arose because UNPROFOR existed to manage a conflict that in, military terms at least, should already have ended, which unfortunately was far from the mark in this case.

The attack on Krajina made the propaganda from both sides even more poisonous. On 6 December, for example, Radio Bihac ran a story that was so unlikely as to be hilarious if they expected anyone to believe a word of it. Briefly, it said that the Serbian escort of a convoy of Agrokomers buses was comprised of high-ranking Serb officers who were met by the Abdic officers with embraces of warmth and affection and glorious words of praise for their Serbian friends. Certain Serb soldiers who saw this display were said to have made derogatory remarks about Abdic soldiers who made no response as, in the words used on the radio, 'they had lost honour and self-respect'. Astonishingly trivial and to anyone with anything between his ears, obviously pure fabrication. Or so I believed. As it turned out, many people on both sides of the line swallowed it hook, line and sinker. It has been said that when war is declared, truth is the first casualty. Never was that more true than in the Bihac Pocket.

On the morning of 10 December, we were on our way to Bihac for our weekly UNMO meeting in sector HQ. About ten kilometres north of Skokovi we came across small groups of women, children and old people, laden with bundles and bags hurrying away to the north. We both exclaimed, as two minds with but a single thought, 'Something's up.' It was like seeing a replay of the situation three weeks earlier when Todorovo was attacked. Five kilometres further on, having passed even more of these small scurrying groups of people, we pulled over to ask a soldier what was going on. As soon as we had got out of the car, the question became unnecessary. About 500 metres to our left there was a long ridge. On the other side of it, heavy fighting was under way. We could hear heavy small-arms fire and a squad of soldiers on standby informed us that the 5th Corps was fighting its way up the other side of the ridge.

The fleeing civilians were still flowing past us, breaking into a trot as they reached the closest point to the fighting, with their loads of personal belongings bouncing on their shoulders like poorly wrapped parcels. Most were frightened, some could not hold back the tears. 'Poor sods,' I thought. Less than two weeks had passed since they had returned to their homes after the last hurried departure, when fears that the attack on Todorovo would spread to the west proved groundless. Now they were on the run again, with the few meagre personal effects they had had to time to gather.

The situation escalated when mortar shells started falling just on the other side of the ridge. Shortly afterwards, the pattern became random and they rained down everywhere as if the bombardiers were just popping in the shells and aiming with their eyes shut. Doubt began to creep in. If the 5th Corps was about to push the Abdic forces over the top of the ridge, the main road would became a battleground and we would be caught once again in crossfire. If we pressed on and the Corps took the ridge we would be cut off. We speculated as to what the situation was like further down the road towards Skokovi. The soldiers we had spoken to earlier told us that this was the closest the fighting came to the road so we decided to continue our journey.

About two kilometres further on, just before the point where the French escort started operating, we met a large group of civilians on the run. One of them was a very large old lady, so unsteady on her feet that she was virtually being carried by the people on each side of her, with her feet trailing uselessly behind. A young man came running towards us, gesticulating wildly with his arms for us to stop. He was hysterical, eyes popping with terror and completely incoherent. 'Take us away from here! Please, get us out of here!' We told him we were headed in the opposite direction and we . . . But he was not listening. He had turned and resumed his panic-stricken run to the north.

When we reached the French escort, its commander told us that the fighting in the area we had passed through had been going on for over two hours but that things were relatively quiet in Skokovi. Thankfully, he was right. We crossed the front line without hearing a single shot. As soon as we had passed the 5th Corps' most forward position, we switched on the radio again and bathed our ears in sweet music. Less than a quarter of an hour ago, we had been just behind the front line, our senses bombarded with the wailing of weeping women and the thundering detonations of mortar shells. Now, peace and beauty. What a strange life we led as UN Military Observers. What contrasts we experienced and how quickly things changed.

A kilometre or so south of Skokovi, we saw a gaggle of people standing and gazing up into the air. We stopped, got out and did the same. *'Avionski!'* (aircraft) – said one of them. He was right. Two Hornet F-18s were circling high overhead like seagulls after the plough, no doubt policing the UN 'no flight zone'. An old man came up to us, stuck his finger skyward and said in German, *'Wann, wann?'* I am sure what he was asking was when NATO was going to start bombing Serb positions, talk about which had been buzzing about for quite some time.

Our meeting over and ready to drive back to the autonomous province, we learned that all traffic via Skokovi had been stopped as the fighting had now spread to that area. We had to take the 'scenic route' instead, through the town of Slunj in Krajina. It was the first time I had taken this route and it turned out to be something of an experience. Not long after we had crossed the border into Croatia – right where the Jordanian had zig-zagged his way through the anti-tank mines – we arrived at the first of countless small villages that had been razed to the ground and abandoned. They were ghost towns without so much as the clucking chicken or barking dog that were so typical of such settlements. We were not surprised to hear from Jasmina that they were Croatian villages. The most badly battered of them was Dreznikgrad which had simply ceased to exist. During World War II it had been known for supporting the *Ustasja* movement, which probably accounted for the thoroughness of its destruction. Jasmina told us that in many places, the Serbs had completely closed off the area, so neither UNPROFOR nor the international press could get in to see what had been done.

It was profoundly disturbing to drive through such horrifying destruction, made even more satanic by the natural beauty that surrounded it. As far as the eye could see, the land was covered in a thick blanket of virgin snow. With the mountains in the background, the scene was just waiting for somebody to come and paint it. Under different circumstances, that is. The stark contrast of beauty and beast and the almost deafening silence sent a shiver down my spine. A few kilometres before we were to drive across the gap in the front at Velika Kladusa into Bosnia-Herzegovina once more, we ran into more devastation in the Croatian village of Cetingrad. Another ghost town devoid of life and movement. For the millionth time, it crossed my mind how many open wounds had to be healed, how many bridges built before the three population groups could live in peaceful coexistence. And for the millionth time, whether it would ever happen.

We made our way straight to Skokovi to get up-to-date with the situation. The situation around the ridge to the north of town was unchanged, with the fighting still going on. At the side of the road sat a group of soldiers recently relieved from their positions on the hillside and resting before being called into the fray again. We asked about the situation around Skokovi but the only answer we were given was that two hours previously the Abdic forces still held the ridge despite repeated 5th Corps attacks. We drove on to see for ourselves and stopped at a car park overlooking the area a couple of kilometres north of the town. We could plainly hear that the fighting had gained momentum, with fire from all sides, but particularly from the east where the mortars were in action. About one round every three minutes was my estimate, and taking into account that neither side had that many mortars at their disposal, that was a pretty intensive rate of fire.

Immediately to the east of the car park was a steep, high and elongated hill. From its top we would be in a great position to observe the heavy fighting we reckoned to be going on a kilometre to the east. A trail led from the car park to a small cottage and we guessed it was only three hundred metres from there to the top of the hill. Joram and I set off but we had not taken many steps before an obviously agitated and nervous man came running out of the little cottage to ask us what we wanted. He urged us not to go up the hill as the Abdic forces had a position up there which, he said, had been repeatedly hit by mortar shells earlier that day. Joram and I debated finding our way to the other end of the hill to avoid running into this position. But time was against us, with only 45 minutes to sunset and neither of us wanted to end up in a situation where we would have to cross an active front line in the dark, which we most certainly would have to do if the Corps managed to fight their way across the ridge they were storming. The jumpy little man interrupted our deliberations constantly and Jasmina, also getting a bit worried, was finding it very difficult to translate his frightened and incoherent stammerings. He cursed the 5th Corps vehemently and claimed they would kill him and his family and burn their house down. He pulled a revolver from his belt, waving it wildly around in the air screaming, 'But they won't get me! I'll shoot the bastards when they come!'

The mortars were getting nearer the car park with every detonation. From the east and the west we heard one explosion after the other getting closer and closer. Suddenly, one exploded only a few hundred metres away. Then another. Then one landed no more than 200 metres away and exploded with a deafening roar. It was a rather persuasive argument that perhaps we should really think about getting home and we hurried towards the car, with the poor, wretched man still babbling about what the 5th Corps would do to him and his family. Just as we were about to set off, he came scurrying over to us and tore open the driver's door. With wild eyes and a demented expression, he was burbling and stammering and desperate about the plight of his family and pleading with us, begging us, to bring an end to the mortar and gunfire. It had probably not been a very effective sedative to see us leaving in such undignified haste. He reeked of *slivovic* and must have been looking for calm and serenity from a bottle or two. The last thing we heard him say was to ask if it were true that we (UNPROFOR) were supplying the 5th Corps with arms. Where such a rumour had sprung from I would dearly love to know. It was certainly no comfort for us, particularly with his state of mind – and the revolver in his belt. The poor man was not being aggressive, just teetering on the brink of insanity and prepared to do anything to defend his family.

We left the car park with the pedal on the metal, heading north for the main road, keeping it there until we reached the ridge that was the topic of conversation for the day. The fighting was still going on, with mortar shells falling with frightening regularity but aimed at a section of the hill some 700 metres away. By now it was almost dark and it was quite a sight to see the tracer cutting the sky into confetti. Next to us, a company of soldiers was taking a rest before returning to the front line. We spoke to the leader, a big athletic-looking man, who seemed impressively bored with the situation and with more than his fair share of the mental equilibrium essential in the warrior. He spoke calmly, clearly and had a ready sense of humour. He had been fighting since the outbreak of war, which went a long way to explaining his ability to accept as nothing the battle that was raging less than a kilometre from where we stood. He was carrying a magazine belt and four small leather pouches, each the size of a clenched fist. Out of the blue, he said 'Fancy a walnut?'

'Um . . . yes please.' He opened the drawstring of the furthest bag to the left and, true enough, it was stuffed with delicious walnuts.

'Or would you rather have one of these?' he asked, opening the bag next to it with a grin and showing us a hand grenade.

He did it with such elegance and dignity and with such an innocent smile on his lips that his odd behaviour seemed perfectly natural. This was a real warrior we were talking to – mucho macho. The harsh realities of war often bring out facets of character that would probably never be seen in normal, peaceful surroundings. For a soldier with war as his handiwork, it is of fundamental importance to test his ability to survive mentally in a combat situation. In past centuries, when soldiers were often at war, the problem did not exist. Nowadays, when there are many places on this planet where war has not been waged for generations there are thousands of soldiers who go through their lives without ever knowing for sure whether they could cope with war if it ever came. Military exercises are no real substitute for the real thing, no matter how realistic the planners try to make them. But most soldiers with a reasonable portion of common sense, are happy not to have to fight a lifetime of battles, everyone of which could rob him of life or limb. This, of course, leaves the modern, professional soldier with a bit of a problem. It is rather like an apprentice bricklayer who has learned the theory of building a house and is confident he can put that knowledge into practice but never gets the opportunity to prove it and therefore never finds out whether his house will stand firm through a hurricane or collapse under the weight of the first fall of snow.

As I was talking to the soldiers, I thought I heard a familiar whistling sound – small-arms bullets whizzing by like angry hornets. As we were quite some way from the battleground, that was quite surprising, but I kept hearing it and soon Joram picked it up too. Where the bullets came from and for whom they were intended we had no idea but it was not a pleasant experience to stand there in the dark and hear these small and fiendish projectiles buzzing about us. With the mortar shells getting uncomfortably close, we made our fond farewells and set off for Kladusa. We arrived, weary and hungry, just as the call to prayer was being intoned from the minarets of the mosques. A long and eventful day was drawing to a close.

The battle for Skokovi continued for some weeks and ended with the 5th Corps gaining control of most of this highland area, which was a decisive defeat for the autonomous province, both in terms of morale and military strategy.

On 24 December, the French Minister of Defence visited the Bihac Pocket to celebrate Christmas Eve with the soldiers of the French battalion. He crossed Skokovi in the morning to call on battalion headquarters on the 5th Corps' side of the front line. In the afternoon he set off with his escorting convoy to Velika Kladusa, where the actual Christmas celebrations were to take place at the battalion's logistics base on the outskirts of town. When the convoy passed the front line north of Skokovi, there was still fighting in the area, which made no difference to the progress of the convoy. The only step taken was to close the hatch on the APC and carry on cooking the Christmas roast. Shortly afterwards, tragedy struck. A sergeant sitting in the passenger seat of an unarmoured vehicle was shot in the right side of the face just under his helmet and killed instantly. His family was informed within two hours. It was a clearly shocked Minister of Defence who held his speech for the assembled soldiers whose Christmas spirit had been so cruelly dispelled.

The French moved heaven and earth to discover what had actually happened. The crucial question was whether the sergeant had been hit by a stray bullet or had been killed in cold blood, and if so, which of the parties was responsible. Everything pointed to the second of the alternatives. The strongest indication was the fact that the large truck had not taken any other rounds. Both conflicting parties accepted that this was probably the most reasonable explanation but both vehemently denied responsibility and placed the blame fairly and squarely on the shoulders of the other side. Neither would accept the blame for this act of murder. The French intelligence unit made use of resources it had installed in both camps and reached the analysis that it was a soldier in the 5th Corps who had pulled the trigger out of anger that UNPROFOR had still not put an end to the arms transport to the autonomous province and still had problems getting food supplies through to Bihac. Whether the sergeant was the victim of the act of a single madman or a planned military action by the 5th Corps as retribution for the failure of the French to bring a halt to arms convoys from Krajina remains an open question. Whatever the case, the location of his killing was a well-chosen site, because for a sniper taking a single shot from the front line with a battle waging, it was child's play to conceal his identity.

With the death of the French sergeant, even the slowest of minds came to accept that our unarmoured vehicles were totally unsuitable for crossing the internal front line. From that day on, our route to and from Bihac was the 'scenic route' via Krajina. That it was a French soldier and not a UNMO who had to lay down his life to prove this blinding fact was a matter of chance. Most of the soldiers in the forward trenches did not know the difference between us and the French battalion, nor care how fundamental the differences in our respective roles. As far as they were concerned, we were all *'Unprofora'*. To them, UNPROFOR was an umbrella for all the international organisations in the area, covering the armed UN forces, the UNMOs, UNHCR and even Red Cross. I have lost count of the number of times I was asked, 'Why don't you carry any weapons?', despite the fact that all parties to the war had been told that there were unarmed, harmless creatures called UNMOs – United Nations Military Observers. However, it was only the senior military officers who understood our autonomy and therefore realised that we were of no military significance. The philosophy of sending us in unarmed, and therefore non-threatening, in order to give us more freedom to do our job was therefore excellent in theory but not always so good in practice.

I celebrated New Year's Eve in 1993 in the company of the other UNMOs in the sector in the town of Cazin, between Velika Kladusa and Bihac on the 5th Corps' side of the front line. It was a wonderful party but on that special night, I felt a long way from home, especially at midnight where, instead of the traditional Danish fireworks, I had to make do with the stuttering bark of automatic rifles from every direction. A few minutes past midnight, the sound of artillery was heard from the direction of Todorovo. It was the Serbs bidding the 5th Corps *'sretna nova godina'* – Happy New Year. Poor wretches, I thought, as the heavy wave of thunder rolled in from the distance. Imagine spending this evening, of all evenings in the year, in a freezing foxhole with artillery shells exploding about your ears. The next morning it was Cazin's turn for a Serb greeting and at 0800 precisely the town was hit by ten shells that set off the air raid alarms. I did not stir, exceptionally, until 1000 and could hardly believe what had happened, what I had managed to sleep through. This brought a smile to the faces of my Muslim colleagues, who must have been more convinced than ever of the satanic powers of the brew they had politely declined the previous night in favour of Coca-cola and fruit juice.

On the afternoon of 1 January, we drove to the Trzac area at the western end of the front line. It was from here that the Abdic forces had launched their attack from Krajina in early December. The autonomous province was in the process of forming a 6th Brigade in this area, according to them consisting entirely of locals and over-spill from 5th Corps. The commander informed us that the brigade's area was the scene of regular skirmishes in and around many inhabited villages which had cost lives. One of the victims had been a 55-year-old man who worked in Slovenia but had made use of the newly-opened bus route between Zagreb and Velika Kladusa to visit his family, whom he had not seen for two years. The family lived in one of the villages where fighting regularly and spontaneously broke out. The last occasion had been the morning of 1 January, when the man, who was not used to diving for cover, was hit by a bullet and killed instantly. He had been gone for two years and home for two days.

The next day, we discovered that a remarkable agreement had

been signed between the autonomous province and the Krajina Serbs, for Serbian forces to reinforce the demilitarised zone of Bos Bojna with military units! This set the alarm bells ringing – Krajina Serb forces re-occupying a demilitarised zone in Bosnia-Herzegovina with the blessing of the autonomous province? How was this possible? was the burning question on all our lips. Delic explained to us at a later meeting that it was the Serbs who had forced the agreement through, in the worry that the province's forces could not protect the Serbs in Bos Bojna against infiltration by 5th Corps troops. He did not appear exactly proud of the situation.

Four days later, on 6 January, a meeting was held at a French observation post in Bos Bojna. The initiative for the meeting to discuss the extraordinary agreement had come from UNPROFOR. The meeting was chaired by a Danish general, military commander of Sector North, who covered the area of Krajina around the autonomous province. Senior officers from both conflicting parties were also present. The meeting began with some comments from Commander Sector North and what he had to say caused quite a stir. He began by saying that General Cot, the French Commander of UNPROFOR, had been quoted as saying that Serbian military presence in Bos Bojna would be a clear violation of international law. So far so good. But, he continued, as UNPROFOR had no desire or intention of being sucked into the current internal conflict[3], it would not take steps to prevent the implementation of the agreement, which should not be interpreted as UNPROFOR condoning the agreement. I glanced across at the Serbian officers to gauge their reaction but they evidently regarded this political distancing as empty talk. They had got what they wanted and anything UNPROFOR might toss on the table would not change things. The Danish general continued by informing the Serbs that if they did start deploying soldiers in Bos Bojna, the French battalion would no longer accept responsibility for the protection of the Serb population in the area. Again, not the smallest of reactions from the Serbs, who saw the French presence as meaningless and insignificant.

I was speechless at what I had witnessed and felt quite convinced that the line of appeasement UNPROFOR had adopted would be very difficult to explain away to the Commander of 5th Corps. Nor would it be any easier to explain to President Alija Izetbegovic, the internationally recognised head of state of Bosnia-Hercegovina – including the Bihac Pocket. He was unlikely to be overjoyed that

UNPROFOR had looked passively on as Krajinan Serb forces rolled into Bosnian territory.

It was not the entire Bihac Pocket that had been declared a 'Safe Area', only an area ten kilometres square around Bihac itself. Nonetheless, it seemed grotesque that the French military presence in Bos Bojna did not make concrete objections to this agreement that was in such violation of international law.

What lay behind UNPROFOR's pragmatic views is, to put it politely, a mystery. But I could imagine that the thinking was that such a tiny geographical area should not be allowed to inflame the Serbs, who could then undermine any possibility of reaching a solution to the problems of Krajina. That the agreement for the re-occupation of Bos Bojna could get off the ground at all, clearly demonstrated yet again that the so-called autonomous province was in reality in the pocket of its Serbian neighbours, who had complete power of decision over its continued existence.

In mid-December, the Sector had welcomed a new SMO who implemented a reorganisation of the UNMO teams in January. As a result, I was transferred on 6 January to one of the teams operating on the 5th Corps' side of the front line, which presented a marvellous opportunity to see the conflict from the other side of the looking glass.

In the almost two months I had spent in the autonomous province, there had been no significant change to the internal front line. The province had won victory in the west but had lost ground to the east and in the centre. It was obvious to all that if the province were to continue fighting alone against the 5th Corps, they would lose. Whether the internal conflict in the Bihac Pocket would turn out to benefit the province depended very much on how much support it could expect from the Krajinan Serb Big Brother next door.

---

1. Hamze was a Muslim warrior and follower of the prophet Mohammed.
2. In 924, Tomislav, leader of the 'principality of Croatia', took the title 'king' and shed the bonds of his Frankish and Byzantine overlords.
3. The proclamation of the autonomous province, the cause of the internal conflict, was the very reason the Bos Bojna agreement could ever become a reality, as the 5th Corps rejected out of hand any thought of relinquishing military control of the area. By quoting the statement that UNPROFOR had no desire or intention of being sucked into the internal conflict, they neatly demolished any objections to the implementation of this remarkable agreement.

## Chapter 12

# *Buzim – In the Company of Knights and Knaves*

As fate would have it, on the 5th Corps' side I came to work with one of the brigades I had heard most about in the autonomous province, 505 Brigade, based in the north-east corner of the Bihac Pocket. Another unit my team was to maintain contact with was 511 Brigade, which defended the towns of Bosanska Krupa and Bosanska Otoka on the River Una, which formed the front line against the Bosnian Serbs in the eastern part of the pocket. The team was based in Cazin, almost bang in the middle of the Bihac Pocket, but according to the new reorganisation plan was due for a move to Buzim at any moment – it had not happened by the time I left at the end of January. Our host family was a kind and friendly middle-aged couple with two teenage daughters. They looked after us and spoiled us dreadfully, providing uncalled for laundry and cooking services during the day and warm company in the evening. The internal struggle was central to their lives, with the husband in charge of an ambulance unit in 505 Brigade and his brother a soldier in the autonomous province. Their jobs were poles apart so the chance of them ever meeting each other face to face in combat was remote – but it *did* exist.

Among my new colleagues was the team leader, Harald, from Norway, and Harris from Pakistan. Harris was a tall, beefy man with a dusky complexion and a large bushy moustache – living proof that the British Raj officer mentality was still alive and well in the far-flung corners of the old Empire. He regarded our host family as our personal servants who should be at our constant beck and call which to my way of thinking, an extremely rude and presumptuous attitude, but to his, perfectly natural.

A few days after my arrival, Harald and I drove to Buzim to make our acquaintance with 505 Brigade. It was a beautiful journey, with forest-capped hills giving way to lush valleys studded with small cottages. Unfortunately, here as elsewhere throughout former Yugoslavia the impression was marred by rubbish dumped blithely where it was most convenient. In places, it formed rotting dungheaps containing everything from kitchen waste to old radios and car wrecks. As breathtaken as I was by the surrounding natural beauty, I was equally stunned by the inability or indifference of these people to appreciate it.

The area around Buzim was the most backward I had seen so far. Many of the small cottages were not made of bricks but wattle and daub (inner skeletons of wood plastered with mud) and had compressed earthen floors. To judge by their appearance and behaviour, the people who lived in them had little or no contact with the outside world. Life went serenely and monotonously on, virtually untouched by the war, apart from the worry and uncertainty that went with having a husband or son at the front. They farmed their postage stamps of land and milked their cows as they always had done, and would continue to do so unless the fighting spread to their peaceful little valley, so much out of step with the rest of their country. It was a black-or-white situation I often saw. The urban or rural population of an area close to the front line had a daily dose of the brutality of life in a country at war, whilst a family only a couple of kilometres behind the lines could live relatively undisturbed, provided the line remained stationary and provided their houses were not in a location that was attractive either as a command post or as cover for a long-range support weapon.

Buzim itself, a small town with a population of a couple of thousand or so, bore the marks of being home to 505 Brigade. The place milled with soldiers, instantly identified by the olive green anoraks peculiar to that brigade. It had a collar with a pale green lining that was left open when they walked around Buzim but laced up when in combat. It was an item of uniform worn with palpable pride proclaiming to the world that the owner belonged to the brigade which Izetbegovic had recently honoured by dubbing it the 'Brigade of Knights' in recognition of their battlefield achievements since the outbreak of war. Its troops were feared by Bosnian Serbs as well as the soldiers in the autonomous province for their dogged fighting spirit. And let there be no misunderstandings – from a military viewpoint, 505 Brigade was efficient and effective. This may or not be why it was not very popular among its comrades-in-arms in the rest of the Corps. If you ever got to know the soldiers from the other brigades even reasonably well, it was patently obvious that they looked upon 505 Brigade as a collection of fanatic, ideological automatons whose concentration on the religious aspects of the war were out of all sensible proportion. Others believed the senior officers of the Brigade used religion as a hypocritical way of motivating their troops without holding any deep religious convictions themselves. When in the autonomous province, I had also heard repeated rumours that this particular brigade mistreated its prisoners.

The soldiers of 505 Brigade were not the only ones to stand out in the streets of the town. Quite a few women, even young girls, wore yashmaks when outdoors, a sight seldom seen among Bosnian Muslims. Many of them had done so on occasion before the war, when religion played a much less important role. It was another indication that Buzim was a place to be reckoned with and the Brigade could hardly have wished for a better group of people from which to recruit soldiers than the backward and ignorant peasant folk. Unlike most of the areas under Muslim control in Bosnia-Herzegovina, the people here appeared intermittently hostile. It was almost as if a spirit of distrust to everything foreign hung over the area around Buzim like a low-lying cloud. Not a single one of the UNMOs was happy to have moved here, with the possible exception of Harris, who disagreed with the antipathy Harald and I shared of Buzim and its ideological brigade.

The brigade commander was a 28-year-old Brigadier-General by the name of Nanic – when the war started 18 months earlier he had been a lieutenant in the JNA. Leaping up the rungs of the military ladder like this was nothing unusual in this war, especially in the Armija BiH, which, without question, was the force with the fewest professionally trained officers at the outbreak of war. At that time, together with two younger brothers he had walked all the way from Split on the Croatian coast to the Bihac Pocket, where his family had its roots. The journey through Krajina had been particularly hazardous and had cost one brother his life. The UNMOs who had had previous contact with the brigade had never met this man as he had always delegated the job to his subordinate officers. But luck was with Harald and I that day, when a messenger informed us that The Boss would like to talk to us. We grabbed the chance and were duly ushered into his office, which was richly adorned with flags, banners, weapons and religious texts framed in glass.

At his desk stood Nanic, about 175 cm with short, dark hair and brown eyes. He would not stand out in a crowd. His greeting was short and sweet 'The name is Nanic. I am the commander of 505 Brigade of Knights. Please be seated.' We were then belayed with the usual lecture on aggressive 'chetniks', the traitor Abdic and other uninteresting drivel. When he had got all this off his chest, he indicated the meeting was over as he had to get back to the front line. We were not given the opportunity to ask a single question and left his office feeling like a couple of errant schoolboys. We promised each other that never again would we accept such bad manners. As it turned out, we never had to, as this was the first and last time we were granted an audience.

I left the meeting with the distinct impression that he was utterly incapable of compromise and totally unwilling to live with someone whose opinions differed even slightly from his own. To use a military vulgarity, he was a real 'shit or bust merchant' who saw everything in black and white and would fight to the last drop of his blood for a Muslim Bosnia-Herzegovina. It became crystal clear that Asim Delic had not been exaggerating when he called Nanic 'the greatest extremist of them all'. I was beginning to think I would leave for home convinced that such officers did not exist in the Armija BiH, despite the stiff-necked claims from Serbs and Croats alike to the contrary.

Harald and I visited the Buzim Brigade on many occasions subsequently and on each occasion we talked with senior officers our patience and self-control were put to the test. One of the worst offenders was the brigade's 'morale officer', responsible for maintaining the unit's fighting spirit. The job was a leftover from JNA days, when every military unit had political officers *à la* the Soviet Army. Now it was not communist ideology that was being preached in 505 Brigade but war against the infidels. His position was made abundantly clear when I asked him what his function was. It was a foolish thing to do. We received a 15-minute sermon, with accompanying chants, which covered a multitude of sins and the importance of religion. I had not heard the like since the heyday of the Ayatollahs. This middle-aged ex-schoolteacher with a grey-white beard addressed us as though we were two menial soldiers in his brigade.

It was, or felt like, a wholehearted and divinely inspired attempt to guide us onto the 'true path', something which Harald and I did not take kindly to. I chose to take it as an experience, intrigued as to how long he could keep it up and how much nonsense he would try and stuff down our throats. It was considerable. But when he started boasting, without as much as a wry smile or a glint in his eye, that the Soldier Knights of 505 Brigade knew no fear, even when under fire by Serb artillery, it was the last straw. The man was an outright fanatic, totally out of touch with reality. The Knave of the Court of Knights.

It was an equally unpalatable experience to meet the brigade's security officer. He was a tall, slim chap of about 30 with cropped blond hair, cold, slightly protruding eyes and a tight smile of doubtful sincerity. He suffered from colossal paranoia, saw 'ghosts' in every corner and steadfastly refused to answer even the most banal of questions 'for security reasons.' His obsessive suspicion assumed grotesque proportions when he once refused to give us a copy of video footage of 505 Brigade that had been shown on Bihac television the evening before. He was also the interrogation officer and therefore, by default, responsible for the atrocities that we were still hearing alleged were being committed in the cellars of the Brigade HQ. That there was more to these rumours than pure vindictiveness, Harald saw with his own eyes on one occasion when he and Harris were in Buzim together. A long staircase led down to the cellar and by sheer coincidence he happened to see three soldiers at the bottom of it beating and kicking a man who was pleading for mercy. When they caught Harald looking at them a few moments later they made weak and stammering excuses that they were just dealing out punishment to one of their own who had kicked up a fuss with a group of civilians when he was drunk on duty. It was such a blatantly transparent lie, Harald did not know whether to laugh or cry.

We repeatedly asked to see the cellar but were turned down every time. Out of the blue one morning, the interrogation officer himself suggested we should inspect the cellars to reassure ourselves their prisoners were being properly treated. The prison cell was a chillingly cold room of about 20m² with grey concrete walls and floor, containing about 25 prisoners. Personal space was, as they say, at a premium. They had been captured some two or three weeks earlier and showed no visible signs of ill treatment. Along one side of the wall there was a row of benches serving as sleeping accommodation. The prisoners sat huddled together on them – the only alternative was the hard, cold concrete floor. They were all wearing an impromptu uniform of sundry articles of clothing so they had apparently been stripped and re-clothed on being taken prisoner, though they all denied the accusation.

To a man, they all professed that they wanted to go back into action fighting for the 5th Corps. After their capture, one of them said, they had come to see that 'the 5th Corps was fighting for the true, just cause'. Another asked me to get a message to the other side – in the autonomous province – and say 'thanks a million for what you have done', a bitter and ironical accusation that they were the cause of the internal conflict. The morale officer had evidently been at work, paying kindly visits and cleansing the minds of these misguided unfortunates, as he would assuredly have put it himself. Next to the door of this cell there was another, securely locked. We asked to see this room too but were disappointed. I would not have been in the least surprised if it had housed the 'wilful children' who refused to accept the true teaching and were referred for 'physical correction' at the hands of the interrogation officer.

We later asked the interrogation officer about the formal status of the Abdic soldiers after their capture. It was obviously not a question that gave him the greatest comfort and he hummed and hahed and gave us a talk on how well they treated their prisoners – so well, many of them changed sides. However, he put his foot in it magnificently a little later when he described the procedure for taking a prisoner captive. After spending a few days of thinking time in the cells, a prisoner was asked if he would be willing to fight for the 5th Corps. If he accepted, he was given a probationary period on the Serbian front. If he declined the invitation, he was brought before a judge and charged with rebellion against the legal government of Bosnia-Herzegovina. Soldiers from the autonomous province were clearly not regarded as regular soldiers of the enemy but rebels and outlaws.

All in all, 505 Brigade, and this officer in particular, did not make the most positive of impressions.

Things were very different when we visited the commander of 511 Brigade, the other unit in our area. He, too, struck me as being a man of iron who had led his command to notable achievements on a very tough front line. But he was a much more likeable and sympathetic character.

The brigade defended an area that included Bosanska Krupa and Bosanska Otoka on the River Una, which formed the front line in the north-east corner of the Bihac Pocket against the Bosnian Serbs. Before we set out on patrol to either of these towns, we always held a meeting with the brigade commander in his headquarters, halfway between the two towns and some distance from the front. The intention was to be given a general briefing on the current situation before driving out with a brigade liaison officer to see for ourselves. We met with him about every third day and on each occasion he reported new losses. One morning he told us with a deep sigh that the previous night they had lost one of their six female front-line soldiers to a sniper in the ruins of Bosanska Krupa's old castle. Female soldiers in support and auxiliary roles behind the front lines were commonplace but female combat soldiers were a very rare breed indeed.

As I had never met one, I asked the brigade commander how they got on compared to their male counterparts. Without a moment's hesitation, he answered that they were highly efficient, cold-blooded fighting machines who managed to stay coolest longest in the worst situations. I must admit that came as quite a shock, but on reflection I could see some form of perverse logic to it. The call-up to Armija BiH did not include women, so the few females fighting at the front line were all volunteers and therefore highly motivated. Those who did choose to wrestle with the validity of the normal and accepted role of women in war were, therefore, most decidedly 'loners' with almost unlimited willpower and gigantic self-confidence.

Bosanska Krupa, like Mostar, was ringed by mountains and bisected by the broad and beautiful river, with water of emerald green, that the Romans had called Una – the only one. Before the war, Krupa had been a popular place for day trips, with the many attractions including water skiing and rowing regattas. It was difficult to imagine that those halcyon days were only a year-and-a-half ago as we stood gazing at the forsaken town centre from the French observation post. The town fanned outwards from each side of the river. On the western, Muslim side it had suffered heavy damage, especially near the mosque which was virtually razed to the ground. The picture told an accurate story of how intense the fighting had been, with infantry battles and hundreds of artillery shells each day. Now it was unusual if more than 20 shells fell a day, though small-arms fire was still an everyday occurrence. In particular, the sharp, loud crack of a sniper's rifle, the weapon that had claimed most casualties in the town.

Just behind the ring of hills that encircled Bosanska Krupa there was a tiny deserted and half-destroyed village. At its centre there was the ruin of a large factory-like building that looked as if it had been demolished with land-mines or dynamite. We asked our liaison officer how this had happened as we knew full well that this area had been in Muslim hands since the beginning of the war. He evaded the question clumsily but finally confessed that it had been a Serbian village whose existence revolved around a *slivovic* distillery which had undergone 'ethnic cleansing' in the early months of the war and been demolished. It was the first time I had seen evidence that this ritual was also practised by the Muslims and although I never harboured any illusions to the contrary, it grieved me to see that in this respect, as in many others, they were little better than the other population groups.

On the return journey from Krupa to Cazin we passed a handful of the black market shops that were so thick on the ground in former Yugoslavia, where there was a shortage of many goods. Each was an Aladdin's cave crammed with everything the heart could desire, from cigarettes and canned food to diesel and diapers. The goods were smuggled in from Krajina along a number of routes and by the size of the organisation, we were talking Big Business. That the smuggling itself and the following sales and marketing activity were conducted in broad daylight was a strong indication that nobody, the authorities included, wanted to put a stop to it. It was as if all concerned were delighted with the fact that although there was a war going on, certain goods at least were still available – provided you could pay for them. In January 1994, a litre of diesel on the black market cost 20 DM, so certain war profiteers doubtless became very wealthy men. As we passed one of these shops, our liaison officer told us with a tone of indignation and resignation that the French paid 40 litres of diesel for a woman. Considering the inflation of black market prices, that was a reasonable price – in Mostar I heard it was three cigarettes. True or not, rumours like this were not good for UNPROFOR's reputation.

Another permanent feature of street life was the hordes of children. Once they spotted our car, they swarmed towards us waving their arms and shrieking *'bon bon'* and *'gummi gummi'*. *Bon bon,* of course, is French for sweets or candy but quite where *'gummi gummi'* came from is a bit of a riddle. The French and our interpreter both said it had no roots in their languages. My guess is that although the children's language tuition was non-existent, there was at least one word of French they knew so why not one word of English – gum. Many of them were admirably single-minded in their quest for sweets, so much so that the bravest – or most desperate for a chocolate fix – put their lives on the line by leaping out in front of our car to make us stop. We knew that many of the parents resented the fact that the war made their children pester us for sweets that they were unable to give them themselves. For this reason, we always went out of our way to make sure we distributed our goodies fairly and correctly to avoid incurring the wrath of sundry mums and dads. To be honest, we also had half a mind on our own safety as we bumped into these fathers on an almost daily basis at the front line. It was a delicate situation, so we were appalled when we saw the French soldiers – in the best traditions of Louis XIV – tossing handfuls of sweets over the outstretched hands of the ecstatic children who would cast themselves headlong into the mud like a rugby scrum to fight for their share. The French set new standards for tactless behaviour.

On 2 January, the conflicting parties surprised us all by agreeing to a ceasefire as the first step in opening negotiations between Abdic and a representative from the government in Sarajevo for a normal-isation of internal relations in the Bihac Pocket. Many of us would never have believed it could have happened and were on tenter-hooks as to how the talks would progress. I tried hard to discover what concessions had been made as a catalyst to end the stalemate situation but found nobody who could give a plausible explanation. It could well be there was none, which would not be the first demon-stration of inexplicable developments in the Bihac Pocket.

By and large, the ceasefire was respected and the talks about talks progressed well under the guidance of the commander of the French battalion. On 16 January, the phone lines were re-opened and two days later the parties signed a document with the grand title of 'An agreement for ceasefire and cessation of hostilities'. The commander of the 5th Corps put his signature on the same piece of paper, bearing the official stamp of AP Zapadna Bosna – The Autonomous Province of West Bosnia – as that signed by, among others, Asim Delic. Although the document did not so much as mention the most sensitive issue, the future status of the province, the very fact that the commander of the 5th Corps would even deign to put his signature to an official document that referred to the province by name was a giant step forward. Until then, the Corps had stubbornly refused to call the autonomous province anything other than 'the rebel region'. There was now a ray of hope for the Bihac Pocket and great expectations of the impending negotiations between Abdic and a Sarajevo spokesman.

Only two days later, however, these expectations suffered a serious setback when the otherwise sensible commander of 511 Brigade dropped the bombshell that the 5th Corps expected to be given full control of the pocket. A non-negotiable condition. He also stated that Abdic was a traitor who should be brought before a military court. At a later meeting with the officers of 505 Brigade and the Corps staff, we were given the same message again, only in much less diplomatic terms. Evidently, the 5th Corps regarded the agreement as an outstretched hand from the winning to the losing side in an attempt to avoid total annihilation of the province's army, with a high casualty rate.

My old team on the other side of the line informed us that the counter-signee to the document put a quite different interpretation on these statements. They saw the agreement as the basis for talks between equal partners – no great surprise there. From that time, we stopped speculating about whether the agreement would hold and started betting on when the fighting would flare up again. The development put us in an uncomfortable position with our landlady who kept pumping us for our views on the likelihood of peace so that her husband could return home.

On 12 January, the day the ceasefire was to take effect from midnight, Harald, Harris and I were once more at 505 Brigade in Buzim. The senior officers were usually reluctant to show us their front-line positions. This time, however, there was a change and we were granted permission to drive to the front line in Todorovo, together with the assistant liaison officer, Nanic's younger brother. The easiest way to get there was to drive north out of Buzim until we reached a small, paved road that led directly to Todorovo. The only problem with this route was that it would take us so close to the front line that snipers from both sides would have a mouth-watering view of our car. This proximity should not have been a cause for concern but we had learned our lesson the hard way and took the twisting earth roads and cattle tracks, up and down the hillsides and across meandering streams that carved their way through the most beautiful countryside in which time seemed to stand still. I had followed the battle for this area from its beginning, right from the time we had talked to Fikret 'Action Man' on the evening before the 5th Corps attacked the town and took him prisoner. I had since observed the fighting on countless occasions but had never been really close to the battleground. And the closer we got, the more excited I became.

Nanic's brother asked us to stop the car just short of a small house to the east of one of the hilltops that surrounded the town. The rest of the journey was to be made on foot. The house had been equipped as a support station, with a small, beaten-up truck with red crescent moons painted on the sides, ready to evacuate wounded 5th Corps soldiers from the battlefield on the other side of a hill just 400 metres away. The other hilltops were in the hands of Abdic troops who thus had a free range of most of the town. They were also in an excellent position to fire on the approach road from the east, the only one available to the 5th Corps – and therefore the one we were about to take.

When we arrived, fighting was already under way, with mortar shells falling in and about the town from all directions. Harald and I therefore thought it expedient to don helmet and flak jacket before continuing, which Harris, as usual, thought totally unnecessary. The first time I had seen him stolidly refuse to take such basic precautions I was puzzled and asked him why. He had looked at me with an expression of bewilderment and, in a tone of voice that betrayed he was just as surprised by my question as I was by his behaviour, said in his lilting Pakistani English, 'It is not up to me to decide when I am leaving this earth. It is the will of Allah. And a flak jacket won't make any difference in that respect.'

It was not the first time I had heard this from Muslim UN officers and deep down I envied them their completely fatalist attitude to life – or death – in which the fate of every individual is predetermined by Allah. Thus equipped, it must be relatively simple to put themselves into dangerous situations which we 'infidels' think it only natural to try and avoid. On the other hand, it was a source of irritation that they neglected to take even the most elementary precautions. After all, if they were to be hit, it would be me that would be left to take care of a mutilated corpse.

From the support station, we set off briskly towards a small cluster of houses, where Nanic's brother made a sign for us to stop. For the next couple of hundred metres we would be visible from a hilltop half a kilometre away where Abdic forces had positioned a clutch of snipers. We covered the stretch in a crouched run, dashing from bush to bush, keeping a watchful eye on our right to make sure we were not leaving ourselves open to a bullet. As I made my headlong rush, I remember thinking how absurd the situation was. The whole point of equipping us with blue helmets and white cars was so we *would* be seen, to make ourselves so visible we would not be taken as a target. Half of me was saying, 'It can't be bloody right that we're sneaking around as if we were combatants,' the other half was saying, 'Shut up and get on with it! You know what life here is all about!'

I kept going and after a while, Nanic's brother called us to a halt again. We were now at the end of a thick hedge, with Todorovo on our left. Our destination lay 50 metres further along the hilltop, a house fitted out as a command post. The Abdic forces were evidently well aware of the fact as it was pitted with thousands of bullet-holes and numerous gaping fissures from armoured shells. Nanic's brother showed us how he thought we should cover the last stretch, which was terribly exposed to fire from snipers and riflemen less than 300 metres away. He took a running start and sprinted, bent over like an arthritic, to the barricaded front door of the house, where two soldiers hustled him inside. We followed one by one at full speed, but not so fast that I failed to notice that the bark of several of the trees I passed had been shot away on the side facing Todorovo.

We were welcomed warmly by the squad of soldiers keeping watch in the command post. Through the gun slits I could see that the two sides were much closer to each other than I had imagined. At these distances, there was no room for error, a second's inattentiveness could be fatal and the troops were constantly on the alert for any new developments. There was a heavy exchange of small-arms fire, with the occasional explosion of a mortar shell and salvos from machine-guns that raked the walls of the house with a series of rapid, loud cracks. The atmosphere in the house was tense and concentrated, but there was no apparent nervousness in the soldiers as they gave us a full briefing on the situation. Afterwards, they invited us to Turkish coffee and for the first time I could remember there was no offer of *slivovic* to help it down – but then this was 505 Brigade, orthodox Muslims to a man.

They fired a number of critical questions at us about the UN's role in Bosnia-Herzegovina in general and in the Bihac Pocket in particular. Although their tone was direct and to the point, it was without any rancour and a lively discussion started about the war generally, which they were convinced would be won at the end of the day by the Armija BiH. One of them said, 'We have a much larger population to draw on and that will make itself apparent as soon as we get the right equipment.' 'If we ever do,' said another, which led to the ever-returning question of the lifting of the arms embargo against the Bosnian Muslims. Everyone knew full well that matters of such pith and moment were decided at a much higher level than ours. Nevertheless, they asked us repeatedly for our personal opinions.

We desperately avoided discussions of this kind as our personal opinions – which were often very different – could easily jeopardise the results we were trying to achieve.

The officers in 505 Brigade, as already stated, were orthodox Muslims and not typical of the Bosnian Muslim population, whose attitude to alcohol, pork and Islam were far too cavalier and very few Muslim UN officers would regard them as 'brothers' in the eyes of Allah. That the senior officers of the brigade had fundamentalist tendencies, or professed to have, was clearly demonstrated a little later when Nanic's brother turned to Harris and said, 'Greet my Muslim brothers in Pakistan and tell them we are fighting well'. Harris mumbled something I could not hear but did not seem to take offence at being included in their 'brotherhood'.

After a couple of hours, we made our thanks and took the same route back to the support station and onwards to Todorovo, where Nanic's brother asked us to drop him at the mosque, as it was almost time for evening prayers.

By far the toughest place in our area of responsibility was Bosanska Otoka, which had been defended with great skill and at great cost by 511 Brigade for more than a year and a half. Otoka lies ten kilometres north of Krupa and is also divided by the River Una which formed the front line, though with Muslims then still holding the odd position on the eastern side of the river. The road to Otoka was long and difficult. It was much easier to take the paved road running alongside the river. Easier but not safer. The French had a particular penchant for this road, despite the fact that every time they used it they were fired upon with small-arms, and occasionally with machine-guns, from the Bosnian Serb positions all along the river. We observers would not fare so well in our unarmoured vehicles so we had no alternative but to take the difficult route that wended its tortuous way through the landscape along pot-holed dirt roads that demanded considerable driving skill in winter. Half a kilometre before the town we always stopped at a sharp bend and put on our flak jackets and helmets. There was a stretch of road from the bend to the town itself that was perfect hunting ground for snipers and machine-guns in emplacements on a hilltop on the eastern ridge of the valley. It was a stretch of road that we needed no second invitation to use as a test track to see what our car was made of.

The western rim of the valley was topped with two high hills, with Otoka itself ensconced in the basin of the valley. The built-up area on the Muslim side stretched from the river half a kilometre up the gently rising western slope. After just a few minutes the town had made its mark as a tough place. Many of the houses were badly damaged, especially on the walls facing east, after the Serbs' repeated battering with mortars, artillery and small-arms. The white façades of innumerable civilian houses were scarred with the dark, round pockmarks of tank shells that were occasionally fired straight at them. The worst casualty was the town's minaret, which the residents believed the Serbs found irresistible for target practice and sighting their weapons. By the countless, and highly visible, direct hits it had taken from top to bottom, it seemed unlikely they were telling fibs. The windows of the the houses had been blasted out long ago and replaced by temporary wooden shutters, hammered over the window frames to protect the inside of the building from shrapnel. The more fortunate houseowners had been able to find thick lengths of heavy timber to clad the eastern walls of their homes as additional protection.

Nobody dawdled in Otoka. Moving from house to house was done at the double to avoid being cut down by snipers who had a free range over most of the town's thoroughfares. These sprinters-under-training included children, their grandparents and mothers who collected water at the few working public taps, all of which were in small-arms range, and then dashed back as best they could, laden with the heavy containers. The eastern sides of the houses were avoided like the plague – people either stayed indoors or stuck sheepishly to the west of their homes. Even the Serb snipers did not shoot to kill with every round, far from it, they did it when the mood took them. It was this constant insecurity that had given the residents a form of locomotion that made them look like hares before the hounds. On top of this fear was the very real danger of being hit by shrapnel from the mortar shells that fell all over town every day at unpredictable intervals, so that nobody could completely relax at any time – indoors or out. This is how the people had been living here from day one of the war and yet the place was still fully inhabited. Not since Mostar had I seen such abject misery as this in Otoka. It just could not get any worse.

A division of French UN troops about 30 strong, manned a permanent observation post in the middle of town, right opposite the mosque. It was hardly a bed of roses. To defend themselves, they had brought with them an armoured scout car armed with an enormous 90-mm gun, making it look more like a tank. This vehicle was like a red rag to a bull for the Serbs, who were none too happy

173

with the French presence in the town anyway. The result was that the Serbs provoked the French daily into returning fire so they could justify an all-out bombardment. To begin with, they had done this by opening fire on the town to discover how seriously the French took their duty of defending the good citizens of Otoka. The French chose to ignore their taunts, most probably because they realised they were hopelessly outgunned if the Serbs used all the weaponry they had available around the town. So to all intents and purposes, Otoka was not defended by the French at all.

The problem was symptomatic of the situation that existed in many of the so-called 'UN safe areas', where the UN simply did not have the hardware to enforce the decision to create some breathing space for the hard-pressed Muslims. To defend the Bihac 'safe area', for example, the UN had only a relatively lightly equipped French battalion of about 1,200 men, which was far too little to provide effective protection, particularly as the battalion was spread across the entire Bihac Pocket, an area of 30 by 50 kilometres. It was always possible, of course, to call up NATO air support, but even so, the UN was far from the powerful force needed for the noble intentions to become reality. As a result, the safe areas were 'paper tigers', existing in name alone, and with the lack of respect they engendered, there was more paper than tiger. This was a consequence the French soon started to feel in earnest. At the French lack of response to the bombardment of the town, the Serbs sent their mortar shells closer and closer to the French observation post. The challenge became more and more open until the provocations had become daily bread.

We patrolled the area around Otoka numerous times and we did not once visit the French observation post without hearing lengthy reports of Serb provocation. They ranged from trivial incidents where they fired over the heads of the French soldiers to more serious actions where it was only by sheer chance that nobody was killed. Only a few minutes before we arrived in town on 17 January, for example, the Serbs had opened fire on the observation post with a cannon. The day before a mortar shell had landed only ten metres from the building. A mortar is far from a precision weapon and the shell could just as easily have ploughed through the roof and exploded inside the house. Despite this awful provocation, the French responded rarely – only when they had been fired on directly and without a shadow of a doubt and then only with weapons of the same calibre or one smaller than those aimed at them. This cautious approach made a mockery of things and meant the UN presence was taken less and less seriously.

Every now and then, the Muslim soldiers charged with defending the town allowed their fury and frustration at the French refusal to retaliate against the Serb bombardment of the town to blow the safety valve in highly dramatic ways. One particular evening after the Serbs had spent the day shelling the town with mortars, a French soldier was shot in the leg as he stood guard outside the building. The French told us later they were quite convinced the muzzle flash had come from the Muslim side of the front line. They complained bitterly to the commander of the Armija BiH unit in question. He promised he would read the riot act and ensure that his troops did not vent their frustration in such a fashion again. Such a promise, however sincerely made, rarely had the desired effect, as discipline among the troops in the forward foxholes, many of them with families in Otoka, left a great deal to be desired. The French were thus in an unenviable position – they had to command respect with extremely limited resources, accept the provocation of the Serbs because they failed to do so and take punishment from the Muslims for the same reason.

On 24 January 1994, I went out on my last patrol. On the itinerary was Otoka, where we arrived at 1100. It really was to be a case of going out with a bang. The situation was very tense and had been since early morning, when the Serbs had fired on Muslim front-line positions and houses further into town. The previous day, they had turned their cannon on the French observation post. The shell had exploded in a room where purely coincidentally there had been no soldiers – had it been manned, they would all surely have perished. Two Frenchmen in the neighbouring room got away with the fright of their lives and a pair of burst eardrums. No sooner had we parked the car and said hello to the officer in charge than the observation post was raked by a salvo from a cannon, whose loud reports echoed round the town. The Frenchmen burst into action and manned their armoured scout car pretending to be a tank and prepared it for action in case the situation should develop into something serious. To the left of the house, a Milan anti-tank missile launcher had been set up in case things really did get out of hand.

I took shelter behind the corner of a house, only to discover a gaggle of children and old people had got there before me. From here, we were safe from direct hits and could still follow the action at first hand. A little boy who was too young to understand what was going on, ran out into the street to continue his play, only to be dragged back with a roar by his mother. At 1102, precisely five minutes after the observation post had been shot at, the turret on the scout car fired two long salvos at the Serbs. A few seconds later we heard two loud smacks as a Serb sniper's rifle sent a couple of rounds into the wall of the house. The French made no reply, deciding to play a waiting game. Time passed with nothing happening and after about ten minutes the people around me began to relax, believing the present danger had passed. *'Kaffa!'* I turned round to see a woman with three Turkish coffees at the ready beckoning the three of us over to a small table in the safe cover of her house. She was offering us not only coffee but *slivovic* and biscuits as well, all three of which must have been difficult for her to get her hands on. It was not the first time we had seen such kindness from the locals, who defied the miserable situation with generous hospitality, though the best they could offer was a cold and battered house, right in the line of Serb fire. That the people of Otoka could even think of being hospitable was beyond comprehension and deeply touching.

After the coffee break, the French officer in charge brought us up to date with the development – as per usual, a lengthy litany of Serbian acts of provocation. As he talked to us we were able to see directly over to the Serb positions that not long before had been meting out their punishment on the town. I let my gaze wander from side to side as I slowly made my way up the hill. I could see several tanks, all stationary but with their turrets trained on the town. They looked like a pride of lions lounging in the sun, waiting to summon up the energy and announce with a roar that this was *their* territory. When we had seen enough, we thanked the French officer and left the observation post for our car. Three steps later, two long bursts from a Serb cannon screamed over our heads and slammed into the wall of the building and we had to bite the dust – or rather cold mud. The Frenchmen made ready to give the usual limited response whilst the good people of Otoka scrambled for cover again until this latest bout of madness had blown itself out and they could poke their heads up until the next one began. As we dashed to the car and drove away, gearbox screaming, I did not envy these poor people. I just managed to glimpse the latest addition to the collection of bullet marks in the already crumbling wall. *'Do vidjenja danska,'* they seemed to say, '*au revoir*, Dane'. Said as only it could be said in Bosanska Otoka.

As expected, the war between the 5th Corps and the autonomous province broke out again a few weeks after I left the Bihac Pocket. The fighting continued through most of 1994, with the Corps conquering the province's seat of government, Velika Kladusa in late August. As a result, thousands of civilians and Abdic troops fled to Serb-controlled Krajina. With the victory, the 5th Corps gained a significant windfall in material and supplies which it put to use some months later by trying to take large areas of territory from the Bosnian Serbs. The attack was repelled, a respite which Abdic made use of when he sent his troops into the pocket from the north, again with Serbian help, in an attempt to reconquer his kingdom. The fighting raged back and forth until August 1995, when the Croatian Army defeated the Krajinan Serb separatists. At a stroke, Abdic lost the power base for his struggle against the 5th Corps. He, and 25,000 Muslims from Velika Kladusa and its environs, fled into Croatia and The Autonomous Province of West Bosnia ceased to exist.

What happened to Asim Delic, chain-smoking Hasan from Vrnograc, Fikret Action Man, the sermonising morale officer, the sympathetic commander of 511 Brigade, and lest they be forgotten, our family in Cazin, I have no idea. However, Buzim will always be remembered as the time I was in the company of knights and knaves.

## Chapter 13

# Zagreb – Thoughts Before the Journey Home

On 25 January 1994, nine months to the day after my arrival, I said goodbye to my host family and drove with Harald to Zagreb where I was to check out (tie up the loose ends with UNPROFOR) before I could get on the aircraft and be homeward bound. At the same time, my landlady, Rabia, also said goodbye to her husband, Hase, who was off to the front in Buzim. It was 15 kilometres away and he would be making the journey on foot unless he was lucky enough to get a lift from one of the few trucks still on the roads in this area of the Bihac Pocket. Hase and I made our fond farewells and wished each the best of luck before he trudged off down the slushy road to Buzim with a bundle of clothes over his shoulder. Rabia was doing her best to be the brave wife and she was fighting hard to hold back the tears. 'When will it all end?' she asked us, and with a woeful expression turned and walked back towards the house. She was given no answer but then she did not expect one. All we could give was a comforting arm around her shoulders and some encouraging words about Hase's speedy and safe return. Of course, we knew as little of that as she did – but it seemed the right thing to say at the time.

Harald and I drove south from Cazin towards Bihac and crossed the front line at the same place as the Jordanian three months earlier had played Grand Prix driver between the anti-tank mines. These had now disappeared, which surprised me rather as there had since been no change for the better in the relationship between the Krajinan Serbs and the 5th Corps. Quite the opposite in fact, with Abdic being given permission from the Serbs to attack the Corps from the rear out of Serb-controlled territory. Hardly what you might call bridge-building tactics.

On the way to Zagreb, we passed one of the INA petrol stations seen all over former Yugoslavia. There was only one pump in operation and from it, a queue of at least 500 people snaked its way along the road. They stood with a motley assortment of tanks and containers, all hoping for a few drops of the precious fluid. So even though Abdic must have had to cough up with a certain amount of the stuff as part-payment for free passage for his goods through Krajina, it was clear evidence as far as I was concerned that the UN blockade against the Serbs was at least pinching, even if it had not achieved the desired effect to the full.

We crossed the front line at the town of Karlovac and the last 50 kilometres of the journey was all motorway. From the exit to UNPROFOR headquarters close to the centre of town, we were given the finger more times than I could count. I had come to believe this was the traditional greeting of the Croatians. Just two hours earlier, we had returned the friendly waves of Muslims we passed on the road and the contrast between them, and the ill-mannered Croats was stark. In the months when snowfall was a regular occurrence, the children of Zagreb had invented a new weapon for use against the UN – snowballs moulded round rocks. If they were delivered with skill, they went straight through the windscreen, as many of our colleagues at HQ knew from experience. It demanded considerable self-control and professionalism not to sink to their level and give them a taste of their own medicine. God, how I wanted to roll down the window and give them an earful they would not forget in a hurry, even if it was in a language where their vocabulary, at least to us, was limited to, 'Fuck you!' Instead I thought happy thoughts, bursting with joy at the fact that I could count the number of days left among these ungrateful and brutish people on the fingers of one hand.

In front of HQ, a makeshift war memorial had been erected, honouring the Croats who had lost their lives since the war began. It was a brick wall, 1.5 metres high and 300 metres long, with every brick bearing a name engraved in white. The ground along the wall was littered with flowers, candles and torches and at the end closest to the main entrance of the building stood a small group of women, presumably mothers or widows, keeping vigil. They uttered no threats and offered no insults but their faces revealed what they thought of the organisation that was represented behind the high, concrete wall crowned with barbed wire.

The daily drudge of HQ was very different from the life I had been living for the last nine months, never far from a front line somewhere. In UNMO HQ, there was a conference room with one end wall given over to maps of the various sectors of the mission area. In this room, a morning briefing of the situation was given every day, collated from the daily reports from the individual sectors. I was present at such a briefing the next morning and for the first time I was able to appreciate the overall picture of the everyday isolated incidents taking place, but I also felt a million miles away from the subject of the briefing, the developments on the various frontal zones over the last 24 hours. Here in HQ, it was neither dank, dirty nor dangerous. The contrast was inescapable to someone recently arrived from one of those sectors where you spent all day gritting your teeth. The information being broadcast in HQ was second-hand information and just that one link of the chain away from the reality of the situation to make it appear different from what was actually happening. This was made abundantly clear to me as the duty officer read the sitrep from the Medugorje HQ, where the UNMOs in East Mostar were reporting for the umpteenth time about sniper fire aimed directly at their building. The way the report was read and the lack of reaction from the senior officer attending the briefing, was ample demonstration that they understood what was happening, but had no earthly idea what the UNMOs in East Mostar were going through in human terms. Many of them had never even been there, hopefully due more to lack of time than desire. This experience served only to strengthen my conviction that it is a fundamental prerequisite for military command that you have to have experienced the harshness of reality at first hand before you are qualified to make decisions affecting other people who are in such a situation. That is far from saying that UNMO HQ was manned entirely by armchair generals, but I most certainly did come across officers whose depth of knowledge and grasp of the seriousness of the situation made me despair.

Sorting out the final administrative odds and ends of my period of duty with UNPROFOR was a relatively quick and painless process, giving me a little spare time to dwell on things and indulge in a little philosophical nostalgia, to collect my thoughts before the journey home. I certainly remember the feeling of emptiness that crept up on me as I sat there, knowing that this chapter in my life had closed. The patrols, the excitement, the uncertainty of never knowing what was going to happen next, the comradeship, the exquisite and indescribable agony and ecstasy of being at the centre of things – all this was behind me. Time had done its astonishing telescoping act, and I would probably never have a second chance to do it better. It was also a source of anguish that the war, the UNMOs, the families and the feuds would continue even though I had left the organisation. The recognition that you are not indispensable, no matter how much of your body and soul you give to a cause, is far from pleasant. I knew before I had left that the good and bad experiences I was taking home with me would never fade – and they haven't.

Although I was sitting there by myself feeling as flat as a pancake, I was still enormously grateful and privileged to have gone through the things I had in the course of those nine unforgettable months. I had taken many calculated risks, sometimes with the most dangerous – and unwanted – outcomes. On the other hand, my experiences – which I would not have missed for all the world – made me a wiser and richer man – richer, that is, of spirit. There was also the privilege not granted to all of seeing the makings of history poured into the mould. I know in my soul that our efforts did make a difference – a difference to many of the ordinary people that are always the greatest victims of any war, and that is something I am rather proud of. Whether my small contribution to UNPROFOR made any difference to the final, overall outcome I cannot say. All I can say it that is was worth the attempt.

As I sat in the UNMO HQ for the last time, relieved of any responsibility towards UNPROFOR, I found myself still observing. Observing my former colleagues going briskly about their work. I did some soul-searching. Would I like to continue in this mission? In a way, unquestionably. Amid the mad jumble of impressions acquired in my time in this place, I knew I was going to miss the excitement and the unpredictability – and it was still calling me. But I missed my family and did not really want to end up putting my life on the line again in one of the other boiling cauldrons of the world. Without wholehearted conviction of what I was doing I would be a danger to myself and to others and so I came to the conclusion that it would be best to go home and let some water flow under the bridge.

Over these last days, my thoughts went to those colleagues who would not be going home from former Yugoslavia. The figures up to 24 January 1994 were 73 UN soldiers killed and 800 wounded. Most of these statistics were generated in Bosnia-Herzegovina but none of the sectors got off scot-free. The loss of every one of those killed is irreparable for their families but compared to the numbers of soldiers who had served with UNPROFOR, the list of dead and wounded was very small compared with what it would have been if they had been combatants. The fact remains however that this mission had claimed far more lives than any other UN operation, and many of the member countries threatened more than once to withdraw their troops if all sides of the conflict did not honour their pledges of guaranteeing the safety of UN soldiers that they had taken before the mandate was granted. What the casualty figures do not record are the thousands of close shaves that the UN forces, including the UNMOs, went through, a few of which are described in this book. It is my impression that, for the UN soldier who had come to within a hair's breadth of losing his life just once, the statistics that showed how dangerous the war had been as a whole were totally meaningless.

As luck would have it, despite having been in many situations that can still make the hair on the back of my neck rise, I came through it all with life and limb. Perhaps the Muslim fatalism is justified after all. On 29 January 1994, I boarded the aircraft for Copenhagen and nine tough, exciting and eventful months of my life in former Yugoslavia had come to an end. As the wheels and flaps came up and Zagreb skittered from sight under the clouds, I sent my colleagues still at war without weapons a parting thought – *'Sretno!'* – good luck to you all.

## In memoriam

For those UN soldiers who did not return home, having laid down their lives to help others, let these words be the last in this personal account of that brutal war:

> Cattle die and kinsmen die
> and so one dies one's self
> One thing I know that never dies
> the fame of a dead man's deeds.

> From the Speech of Odin
> in the Icelandic prose narrative, *Poetic Edda,*
> recorded in 1220 by the historian Snorre Sturlason.

# Postscript

The war in former Yugoslavia, as everyone knows, did not come to an end with my departure. In Croatia, where HV had become a force to be reckoned with, despite the arms embargo, the government took matters into its own hands and defeated the Krajinan Serb uprising in Sector West in the spring of 1995. This may just have been a kite-flying operation, who knows, but a few months later, in early August, the Croats launched a major offensive called 'Operation Storm'. In just three days, they took control of the remainder of Krajina, with the exception of East Slavonia. On the radio, President Tudjman promised them amnesty if they would lay down their arms. Whether he really wanted them to stick around is anybody's guess, but a flood of refugees the like of which had not been seen since the outbreak of war followed in the wake of the offensive. This time, however, it was Serbs fleeing in their tens of thousands into Bosnia-Herzegovina. Before long, UN reports of systematic destruction of Serbian property began to appear, which inevitably reminded me of what I had seen in the Medak Pocket.

The Croatian attack produced little reaction, either from Serbia or the international community, which in reality accepted that Croatia was doing the same as the Krajinan Serbs had been sanctioned for some four years earlier – making it difficult, not to say impossible, for the other population group to live in the area. The lack of international response is probably due to the fact that Croatia had excellent relations with the west and its hope that without the problem of the Krajinans, Croatia would be able to devote itself to solving the intricate war in Bosnia-Herzegovina.

Whatever the circumstances may have been, the repossession of Krajina meant a serious loss of prestige for the UN. Its thousands of troops were in the area with the express purpose of ensuring that Krajina was not lost to military force. That they were unable to solve

183

the conflict in Croatia for various reasons, some of them entirely beyond their own control, tarnished its already dulling sheen of credibility and the most pessimistic are now mumbling in their beards that the organisation is digging its own grave.

The war in Bosnia-Herzegovina continued, despite several peace initiatives from UN and EC statesmen. Ceasefires were agreed upon – and violated. A so-called contact group, consisting of representatives from the four major European powers and the USA, assumed international leadership.

In July 1995, the Bosnian Serbs attacked and conquered the UN safe zones of Srebrenica and Zepa, which for once and for all revealed they had been safe by name alone. Thousands of Muslims were 'cleansed' and sent packing to Tuzla. The Serbs stuck two more fingers up at the international community by attacking the Bihac Pocket on all flanks and refusing entry to the convoys of help and supplies. They justified their actions by claiming the safe zones had been used as bases for the government army's attacks against the Serbs, naming the offensive launched from the Bihac Pocket in the autumn of 1994. As usual, the latest outburst of Serb aggression was condemned by the international community, a public outcry of indignation which, as usual, went no further than words.

The last straw that broke the camel's back however, came in August 1995, when a Serb shell fell on the market-place in Sarajevo and killed 40 people. Massive NATO bombardments were ordered against the Serbs in the area around Sarajevo and other places in Bosnia-Herzegovina in an attempt to force the Serbs to the negotiating table. The basis for peace talks was still the plan that divides Bosnia-Herzegovina into two regions, with 49% to the Serbs and 51% to the Muslims and Croats. The borders specified in the plan had been rejected several times by the Serbs.

In the first half of September 1995, the Bosnian Muslims took advantage of the softening-up the Serbs had suffered after more than 3,000 NATO attack missions and in the space of a fortnight took 20% of south-west Bosnia-Herzegovina from the Serbs. The offensive was successful thanks to huge support from the regular Croatian Army, who on Alija Izetbegovic's invitation intervened in the war. Later in the same month, the Croatian Army attacked the Serbs from the north through the former DANBAT (Danish Battalion) area. The UN Security Council spoke ill of the offensive but did not condemn it. Bosnia-Herzegovina's Foreign Minister classified the action not as an act of aggression against his country but its liberation. The Muslim-Croat offensive continued and towards the end of September the Serbian stronghold of Banja Luka was under real threat. At that time, the Muslims and Croats were in control of more than half the territory being fought over. Izetbegovic threatened to attack the town unless it was demilitarised – a not unknown threat in this war, where the winds of success were now blowing from a different direction.

On top of these dramatic developments, a ceasefire came into effect that paved the way for three weeks of intensive negotiations in Dayton, USA, where the presidents of Croatia, Bosnia-Herzegovina and Serbia reached a peace agreement in November 1995. Tudjman and Milosevic negotiated for the Bosnian Croats and the Bosnian Serbs respectively. Under the Dayton Accord, Bosnia-Herzegovina will continue in existence as a state divided – a Bosnian Serb republic, with 49% of the land area and a federation of Croats and Muslims, with 51%. Divided or not, certain functions will be centralised, parliament and the system of justice to name but two. Time will tell whether the first real chance of lasting peace in this war-ravaged country will be taken.

A NATO force of 60,000 armed soldiers replaced the UN troops in order to ensure the realisation of the treaty. By then, UNPROFOR had served its purpose and this would be a fitting moment to remember the more than 180 UN soldiers who were killed and the almost 1,700 who were wounded in this, the largest UN mission ever.

On a personal level, adapting to a very different lifestyle in the safety and comfort of home was not without problems. Having been in the thick of things every day, for better or for worse, observing the worst conflict on European soil in half a century, life at home can sometimes seem banal and uneventful – a trivial pursuit. Things I used to see as problems or challenges now seem to be little more than bagatelles and it can be difficult to see why other people do not think the same. Having seen people collect water at a tap at the cost of their lives in East Mostar or kin fight kin in the Bihac Pocket, I find it difficult to get excited about many of the storms in teacups of domestic – and Danish – life.

It has been very difficult to suppress the emotions of the harsh experiences that are still uppermost in my memory. I am not haunted by them – I have no psychological or emotional scars from what I went through. I have come home with the belief that if you have ever been somewhere and seen *what* happened, *as* it happened, your soul never quite leaves the place. In particular I think about what may have happened to all those people I met. I have not forgotten them and hope they will not forget me. For some reason I am quite convinced we will meet again when it is all over.

# *Maps*

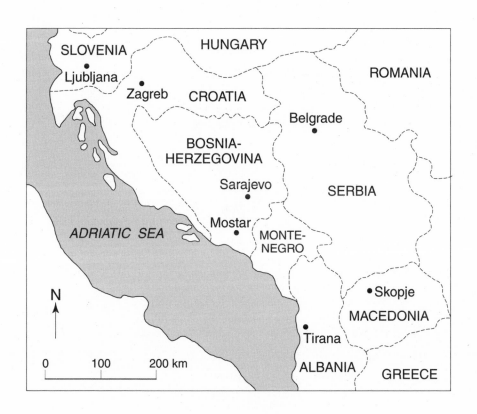

Former Yugoslavia

187

Croatia, showing Serb-controlled Krajina

Areas of operation mentioned in this book

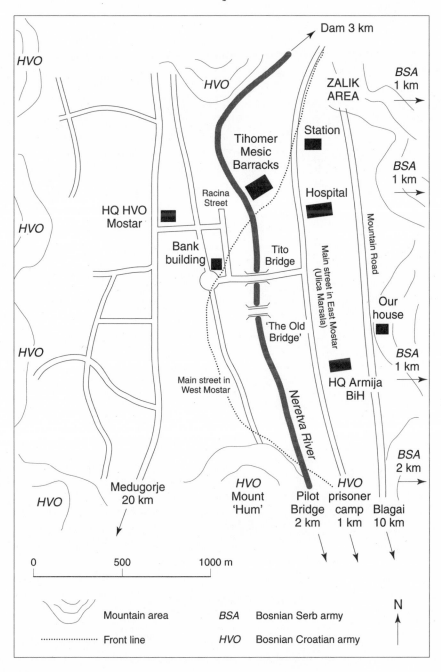

Plan of the Mostar Battle in May to June 1993

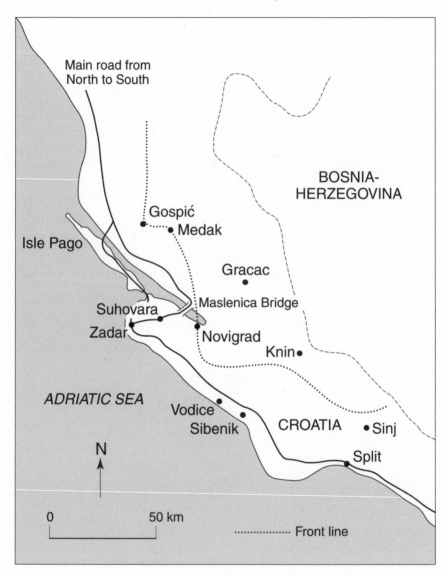

Sector South, August to October 1993

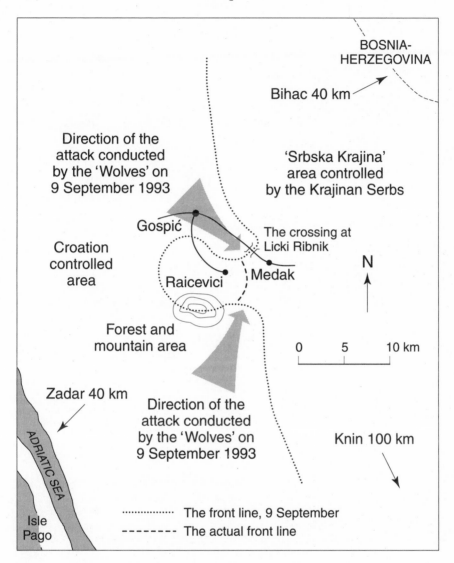

The Medak Operation, 9–17 September 1993

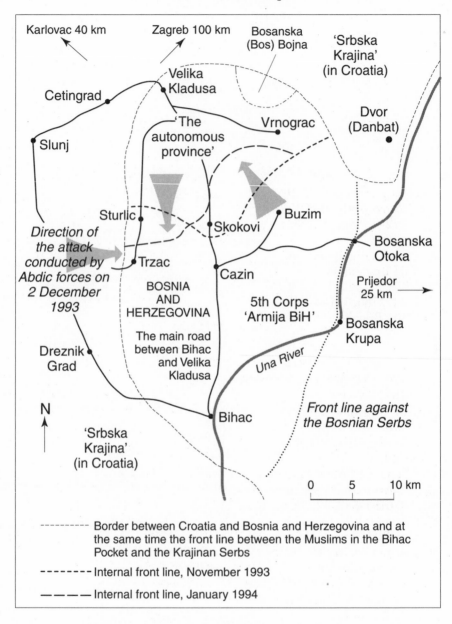

Karlovac 40 km

Zagreb 100 km

Bosanska
(Bos) Bojna

'Srbska
Krajina'
(in Croatia)

Cetingrad

Velika
Kladusa

'The
autonomous
province'

Vrnograc

Dvor
(Danbat)

Slunj

Sturlic

Skokovi

Buzim

Bosanska
Otoka

*Direction of
the attack
conducted by
Abdic forces on
2 December
1993*

Trzac

Cazin

Prijedor
25 km

BOSNIA
AND
HERZEGOVINA

5th Corps
'Armija BiH'

Bosanska
Krupa

The main road
between Bihac
and Velika
Kladusa

Una River

Dreznik
Grad

N

Bihac

*Front line against
the Bosnian Serbs*

'Srbska
Krajina'
(in Croatia)

0      5      10 km

--------- Border between Croatia and Bosnia and Herzegovina and at
the same time the front line between the Muslims in the Bihac
Pocket and the Krajinan Serbs

-------- Internal front line, November 1993

— — — — Internal front line, January 1994

The Bihac Pocket, November 1993 to January 1994

# Index